THE NOBLE CFO

HOW TO START AND GROW A FLOURISHING CFO BUSINESS

ART ZYLSTRA

FOUNDER CFO BUSINESS PARTNER

INDIE BOOKS
INTERNATIONAL®

ISBN-13: 978-1-952233-73-9
Library of Congress Control Number: 2021916727

Designed by: Joni McPherson

INDIE BOOKS INTERNATIONAL®, INC.
2424 VISTA WAY, SUITE 316
OCEANSIDE, CA 92054

www.indiebooksintl.com

DEDICATION

Many people have influenced and impacted my life in various ways. Each of these people have played a part in shaping and molding me to be the person I am today. There is not room on this page to acknowledge them all.

To my parents, Clarence and Theresa Zylstra, who did not live to see me write this book, for instilling in me a work ethic and a desire to volunteer in the community.

To my wife, Ronda Zylstra, for her patience with me as I traveled, got my degrees, volunteered, all while we raised three children.

To my children, Clayton, Kari, and Laura, for helping me be a better parent.

To Bakke Graduate University for giving me the words and platform to build on my stewardship theme.

To Michael Oskouian, a friend, mentor, and the person who encouraged me to expand my business, as a way to reach more business owners with my message.

To Henry DeVries, who was instrumental in guiding me through writing this book.

TABLE OF CONTENTS

CHAPTER 1

Why Start A CFO Business

> *The only way to do great work is to love what you do.*
> *If you haven't found it yet, keep looking. Don't settle.*[1]
> —STEVE JOBS

Do you work with a mission-driven company that aligns with your values and your dreams? Are you being paid for the value that you bring to your employer?

You have worked hard to build a career in the corporate world. Businesses need your insights and expertise. Owners you have worked for have built successful companies and wealth. Accomplishments like this should define a successful and satisfying career for most accounting and finance professionals. And yet there still is this nagging thought in your mind that asks, "What am I missing? Why am I not more satisfied with my career?" In the following chapters, I will lay out an alternative career path that, if followed, will allow you to experience the satisfying and well-paid career you have always dreamed of having.

Perhaps you have committed to spending more time focused on your family and not climbing the corporate ladder. Good for you. But now you are looking at your retirement funds, and you realize that being family-oriented has had an impact on your career earnings. Or you have helped owners accomplish their dreams at the expense of putting your life vision on the back burner. Sure, each business you worked with created jobs in the community, but did you have a sense of pride in the company's mission? How many times did you feel pressure to make decisions that did not align with your values? What dreams have you given up on to pursue your career? I have experienced each of these questions throughout my career. My quest has been to find a job that provided me with career satisfaction and a sense of accomplishment without sacrificing my integrity and a salary I could build a retirement on. However, each position has left me with the same question, "What am I missing"?

I thought that my last W-2 job checked as many boxes as possible on the career satisfaction indicator. I had always looked at my career as a means to do the things that I truly enjoyed doing. As long as my job allowed me the capacity to spend time with my family, travel, educate myself through reading, and impact the community, that is all I needed. Bakke Graduate University (BGU) was the dream job that combined all these desires and packaged them in a job. I was confident that this would be the job that carried me to retirement.

BGU is a mission-driven organization leveraging a global network of leaders and partners to deliver a values-based education to urban students worldwide. BGU combined a whole-church theology with a quality academic discipline designed to empower the underserved to transform unjust laws and oppressive public structures. BGU recognized that local and global business has a growing influence in our world and an increasing crisis of purpose and ethics.

The mission of BGU was a perfect fit for me. I love to travel and experience different cultures around the world. I believe that the unity of faith-based organizations collaborating with values-driven businesses can transform communities in ways we can only imagine. I know that contextual and experiential education rooted in today's global realities will have a community impact.

The work environment at BGU was collaborative and included clerical, teaching, and leadership in all educational processes. I knew I had found a home when I learned that the department, traditionally known as Human Resources, was called People Development. One of the founders of BGU began to refer to me as the Chief Stewardship Officer instead of Chief Financial Officer. This label was an affirmation that the culture of BGU was the right place for me.

Could it be possible that I finally had found a job that checked all the boxes for what I was looking for in a career? I enjoyed working with the staff at BGU. I was developing authentic relationships with students and staff alike. I was able to operate in integrity in fulfilling my duties as CFO. Stewardship was an essential value of the school, and I was able to follow an extraordinary path of stewardship. Pursuing an attitude of service was honored, encouraged, and highlighted through the principles of servant-leadership. Each staff member and each student was valued as an individual pursuing their path of accomplishment. Mistakes were considered opportunities to learn. Operating in grace was standard practice.

Had I discovered the holy grail of jobs? A mission and values-driven organization that valued and developed people was as good as it gets, right? Other than the forty-minute commute into the city, it was perfect. Oh, and getting paid at the bottom of the pay scale for a CFO role. Not to mention a business model highly dependent on the contributions of a few major donors. In the end, donor money dried up during the recession of 2008, and the university had to lay off many of its staff, including myself. BGU was forced to reinvent itself and since that time BGU has moved locations, developed a new financial model, and is now a vibrant global university. Yet as they spent a decade reinventing themselves, I also had to invent a new way to use my gifts and calling in ways that created value for others while providing financial sustainability for my family.

What I learned from this experience has shaped and molded my path forward in launching CFO Business Partner. I knew it was possible to run a successful business by operating on the values that were important to me. What I wanted to add to the mix of working with a values-driven company was the opportunity to earn a salary that was on the higher end of the pay scale. I also wanted to have more control over my work schedule. I envisioned eliminating the daily commute into the city and having a work time that flexed with my interests outside of work. The solution for me was to start a CFO consulting business. This book will show the reader what fuels the success of CFO Business Partner and how you can launch your own licensed CFO Business Partner practice.

Today's business world is rapidly changing. Corporations are beginning to realize that the big corporate headquarters is becoming an obsolete business model. While not all employees have the skills and personality to work from home 100 percent of the time, most can spend at least a part of the week working in a home office environment. Companies are discovering that productivity is going up without micromanaging employee schedules. Businesses are increasingly becoming more comfortable with staff working remotely. The economy is forcing enterprises to consider layoffs and downsizing, especially in corporate administrative roles. What a fantastic opportunity to fill the gap as a gig worker. Recent surveys show that 25 to 35 percent of workers earn at least a portion of their income from freelance work. The gig economy is not made up of just lower-skilled services. A U.K. research revealed that 59 percent of the U.K. gig economy was made up of knowledgeable and professional workers.[2]

According to a survey by Eden McCallum, 90 percent of independent consultants are satisfied working as consultants.[3] The vast majority of these workers are more satisfied with their current professional lives then they were as employees. They are earning more or at least the same as when they were employed and working fewer days. This survey data suggests that independent working is satisfying because the work is more meaningful and has a significant impact. The consultants surveyed report they have more control over their time and more flexibility in balancing their work and personal lives.

What are the reasons that stop so many W-2 finance and accounting people from starting their own consulting business? The personality traits that make for good accountants are the same traits that cause fear, anxiety, and doubt with starting a business. The Myers-Briggs Type Indicator test gives us some clues.

Most accountants have introverted personalities. This means they draw energy from being alone. Building a consulting business means networking and meeting people. Thoughts go immediately to the pushy salesperson that no one likes. This alone can be a deal-breaker. This is a valid concern, and anyone considering starting their own business must be resolved to push past the desire to network exclusively through email and social media.

I have found that networking is energy-draining; however, I also enjoy meeting people and listening to their stories. Networking does not have to mean being pushy and obnoxious. Here is the secret: the people who will be best at finding clients for you are extroverts. Extroverts love to talk. When I network, I ask a couple of leading questions and then sit back and listen. It is incredible how many extroverts think I am a great conversationalist and good friend because I am a good listener. I have used my introverted personality as a strength in developing friendships and building trust. Building trust brings leads and clients. This seems counter-intuitive, but it works.

Another barrier is that most accountants rely on concrete, tangible evidence to make decisions. They are logical and use facts and numbers, rather than intuition, to guide their life choices. The facts from the U.S. Bureau of Labor Statistics say that about 20 percent of U.S. small businesses fail within the first year. By the end of the fifth year, roughly 50 percent have gone out of business, and after ten years, about 65 percent have failed. The logic might suggest not to start a business out of fear of failure. The entrepreneur uses business failure as a catalyst to success. The accountant uses the potential of business failure as a reason not to go out on their own. This is reasonable and logical thinking.

You are considered accountable, dependable, and diligent. You make good decisions based on analyzing data. This is a strength that will help you be successful with a consulting business. According to the U.S. Small Business

Administration, there are approximately 31.7 million small businesses in the United States. Consider how many of these companies cannot hire a full-time CFO but need the CFO expertise to guide their financial decisions. The data suggests that the demand for outsourced CFOs is great, but the supply is small, simply because the accountant's personality is a barrier to entry. Run the numbers and consider how many clients you need to make a good living. As the CFO of your own business, how should you advise yourself to look at this business opportunity?

The accountant personality enjoys structure and stability. A consulting business feels unstructured, and income streams seem unreliable. Consultants often work on project-oriented jobs. When one project is done, then another one must be found to have consistent income. Too much time in between projects can be devasting from a financial perspective. Business development is energy-depleting and runs counter to the accountant's personality. Predicting variable revenue streams is the bane of accountant's work. How does one project income and expenses when the revenue is hit and miss? Business owners spend sleepless nights worrying about meeting payroll when sales fall off. Why would I want to put myself in that position?

The business model that I have created is all monthly-recurring, flat-billing, predictable income. Every month I provide consistent and predictable reports and work for my clients. I bill them the same amount each month, and they are happy to send me checks, knowing there will not be any billing surprises. This business model builds in the structure and reliability that fits my personality and the consistent billing that my clients need to manage expenses.

The thought of starting a consulting business can be an anxiety-producing process. There are many reasons, from a traditional accountant's perspective, that are valid to decide not to go out on one's own as a freelance consultant. However, we know relying on old data is misguided. The world is changing how we do business and, as accountants, it is prudent for us to begin thinking outside of the traditional box. The accountant's personality has many strengths that will serve the new gig economy well.

Do you work with a mission-driven company that aligns with your values and your dreams? Are you being paid for the value that you bring to your employer? Are you still being nagged by the thought in your mind that asks, "What am I missing? Why am I not more satisfied with my career?" I have heard it said that the right career creates a state of mind that transforms your life. Having a deep connection with your career motivates you to higher levels of success and satisfaction. Suppose this message of pursuing a noble CFO business career path resonates with you. The following chapters will explain how becoming a licensed CFO Business Partner will give you the confidence to live out your dreams.

CHAPTER 2

How To Create A Lucrative and Recurring Stream Of Revenue

Try not to become a man of success.
Rather become a man of value.[4]

—ALBERT EINSTEIN

Accountants like to have a road map on where to go and how to get there. They are looking for structure and support in what they do. Before they start their own businesses, people with the accounting-type personality will likely look for an opportunity with a detailed how-to manual. Franchises are popular businesses to start because of the structure and training. A franchise investment offers a ready-made business model, along with training, guidance, and support. Franchises have detailed instructions on how to run the business and where the location will be. The owner is required to follow these protocols and has the privilege of paying a royalty fee to associate with the corporate franchise. Joining a franchise might be the best route to go for some people to start a business. There are a variety of franchises that are accounting-, bookkeeping-, or tax return-oriented. I would ask you to consider the question at the beginning of this book: "Do you work with a mission-driven company that aligns with your values and your dreams?"

> *If an opportunity is not aligned with what matters most to you (your core values), let it pass. The opportunities that don't make your soul sing, or that you can't be excited about, just end up taking space where a better opportunity could be. Don't settle for something fine—wait for something great!*[5]
>
> —LEANNE JACOBS

The Noble CFO is not a step-by-step guide on how to be a CFO consultant. Many books will give you insights into owning your own consulting business. Numerous books are explaining the intricate details of how to network and how to market your consulting business. I did a Google search for "Consulting Books," and it showed 52,000,000 results. Searching for "Best Consulting Books" narrowed my search to 42,200,000 results. I am a huge advocate for reading, learning, and improving my skills, but how do you narrow your choice of resources down from 42 million results?

The best-sellers in the business book category generally cover broad, over-arching themes that translate well into any business environment and life in general. Books such as *The Trusted Advisor* by David H. Maister, *How to Win Friends and Influence People* by Dale Carnegie, and *Good to Great* by Jim Collins are on most M.B.A. program-recommended reading lists. What makes these books unique and enduring? Here are some testimonials from well-known and respected businesspeople.

The Trusted Advisor: "This book is engaging, enjoyable, and absolutely on target. It is packed with truth. The Trusted Advisor will guide success not just in the advisory professions but in leadership and life as well." (William F. Stasior, Senior Chairman and former CEO, Booz-Allen & Hamilton)[6]

How to Win Friends and Influence People: "It changed my life." (Warren Buffett)[7]

Good To Great: "This carefully-researched and well-written book disproves most of the current management hype from the cult of the superhuman CEO to the cult of IT to the acquisitions and merger mania. It will not enable mediocrity to become competence. But it should enable competence to become excellence." (Peter F. Drucker)[8]

The Noble CFO may not end up on the Ivy League's M.B.A.-recommended reading list, but the philosophy behind how to become a *noble* CFO is the same as the best-selling books listed above. You know the technical aspects of being a controller or CFO. You understand financial reports, cash flow statements, KPIs, and metrics. The secret to my long-term success as an outsourced CFO is living out the six values that I have identified as mission-critical to my business:

1. *Develop authentic relationships.* Human beings are naturally wired to desire relationships. When we meet someone for the first time, our brains unconsciously search for clues to determine whether this person is trustworthy and authentic. Establishing authentic relationships in business is not just a feel-good trend. Authentic relationships enable people to connect personally with you and your business, which leads to a more fruitful relationship. Each person seeks to gain a fuller picture of the other person. When you know someone personally, you will better understand what motivates them professionally and encourage your prospects and clients to engage with you and become your ambassadors. It brings a level of substance to your services that elevates your business above the competition. Your brand is identified as influential, reliable, and trustworthy.

2. *Operate in integrity.* Integrity is the quality of being honest and having strong moral principles. Integrity demands that we do the right thing because it is the right thing to do. Recognized and respected leaders

do everything in their power to follow through on the promises they have made. Telling the truth is not always the easiest thing to do, but leaders with integrity are not afraid to face the truth. Integrity also means that a leader will acknowledge that they could be wrong. Integrity in business is an essential ingredient for sustainable, long-term business growth and success. It can be hard to define and difficult to measure, but you know it when you see it, and it's clear when it's not there.

3. *Follow extraordinary stewardship.* Stewardship is the conducting, supervising, or managing of something entrusted to one's care. Stewardship asks us to be deeply accountable for the outcome of our client's organization. Service over self-interest is stewarding people by giving away power to allow lower-level employees to make important decisions about the organization. Following extraordinary stewardship in business is seen in a company that generates a reasonable profit, develops the people who work for it, treats clients and vendors with respect, and is proactive in investing in the community. This stewardship creates a healthy ecosystem for all to flourish.

4. *Pursue an attitude of service.* The qualities associated with strong leadership and sound management in a business seldom include an attitude of service. Executives in a position of power would look at

servanthood as a weakness and below their dignity. This is incorrect thinking. Pursuing an attitude of service is a characteristic of success for many businesses. They have a people-focused culture that ensures meaningful stability during times of rapid change. Many business thinkers and writers recognize the value of servant-leadership. The attitude is increasingly relevant to the challenges in today's business.

5. *Value the individual.* The fundamental importance of democracy is that every individual matters. No matter what walk of life a person comes from, each opinion and voice is unique. A business should treat every individual it interacts with in a way that values their dignity and worth. When a company values the individual employee, the criteria for organizational performance and success are not measured primarily in financial terms. Instead, the workplace is filled with joy for the ordinary worker and is measured by the worker's quality of life. Leaders that have a passion for people and value each individual will find joy at work as well.

6. *Operate in grace.* Grace in business is a virtue that treats others with respect and dignity. Grace encourages business associates and is a source of positive energy. I love the concept of grace in business. It is a beautiful principle. I have worked

my whole career with this principle in mind. If I show people they are appreciated, valued, and heard, they inevitably work harder and try their best to live up to expectations. Extending grace gives the gift of dignity. I treat each person as a person and not as an object or asset. Each person I interact with in business is a person with dreams, feelings, and needs. Grace is about extraordinary stewardship of authentic relationships developed and operating in integrity, with an attitude of service, placing value on the individual. This is grace in business.

Leaving my dream job at BGU was a painful experience. I was tired of the ups and downs of the W-2 job. I seriously doubted that I would find another job that was as fulfilling as my last. I began applying for several different CFO and director of finance positions with local non-profits. The result was the same: no interview, no job offer. I was nearing my mid-fifties, and I was beginning to feel the effects of age discrimination, but there was never real evidence to prove it.

My thoughts began drifting back to the times I had attempted to start my own business. I did not feel like I had the luxury of time to invest several years in a company that ultimately might not end up being successful. Yet, I was far from having the resources to retire, and I was not having success in finding a W-2 job. What could I do that would leverage my thirty years of experience, minimize the risk of not being successful, and provide me with a sense of fulfillment?

The first place I began to look was at the possibility of owning a franchise. I knew that owning a franchise could increase my chance at success. I had done some investigating into franchising several years before and thought this might be a good way forward. My financial planner encouraged me to consider becoming a certified financial planner with Edward Jones. He had done a mid-career switch to financial planning, and after several years of hard work, it was beginning to pay off for him. Edward Jones provided training, an office, and a minimal salary to start. The more I thought about this opportunity, the more I realized that I did not want to learn a whole new discipline of work. This was not my passion or my expertise, and so I rejected the idea. Next, I spent some time looking into bookkeeping franchises and tax preparation franchises. I would be able to leverage my expertise and not incur a large learning curve. I began picturing myself operating this type of business. I was not able to feel a passion for either one of these businesses. I did not want to settle for a business that fit what I could technically do, but which did not feed my passion for making a major impact on the business world.

Several years before leaving BGU, I had looked at the opportunity of becoming a contract CFO. There was a firm I had investigated that provided sales training and a template on how to make pitches to business owners to become their contract CFO. The introductory price was a little steep but still less of an investment than many of the franchises I had looked at. The royalty percentage on earned revenue was similar to other franchises. I would become a partner of the firm and own my book of business. The opportunity checked most of the boxes that I was looking for. It had some structure, some training, some mentoring, and some autonomy in finding and working with my own clients. The main limitation was I would still be trading my time for dollars and not building a business that leveraged my time. That was an acceptable tradeoff for a limited-dollar investment and the potential to double my W-2 earnings.

I decided the time and the opportunity were the right fit for me. I still had several months of unemployment that I would be able to collect while laying the groundwork for this new venture. I was able to convince my wife that this would be a business in which I would be successful, and that would allow me to earn more money than I ever had at my W-2 jobs. I did my due diligence in talking with other partners of this firm, lined up a mentor, established my goals, and wrote the check.

I ultimately decided to leave the firm I was with to launch out on my own and establish my own brand. I am passionate about bringing stewardship and grace into the business world. The firm I was with only focused on how to make as much money as you could from businesses. The focus was on finding projects that could be billed by the quarter-hour.

There was zero emphasis on the values that I believed were important to build a successful and sustainable business. CFO Business Partner has a message for the business world that needs to be told. My goal for this book is to invite you to join me in this journey to transform the business world. Let us together show the world that being a CFO is a noble endeavor that has the potential to be a transformational agent for good for business and our communities.

CHAPTER 3

Develop Authentic Relationships

In today's business environment, we see a variety of different leadership styles. The Industrial Revolution introduced an authoritarian style of leadership to the manufacturing world. This style was accepted as the best way to get the necessary work done with people who did not enjoy their jobs. The 1990s saw a shift to what some are calling the Relationship Era. Business leaders realize that authentic relationships are a vital element in building trust with employees and customers. Conflicts are being resolved through relationships instead of the boss using their authority to end the conflict. Authentic relationships mean being honest with someone while being vulnerable. It is the ability to share your ideas and who you are without fear of being judged by others. Without vulnerability, trust and connection with others does not happen. Authenticity and vulnerability are directly connected.

Authentic Relationships: A Deeper Look

Human beings are complex creatures. When two human beings meet for the first time, research suggests that our brain begins to look for clues about whether the person we just met is trustworthy enough to start a conversation with.[9] I have met many people throughout my life, and there are some people that I naturally connect with and others that I have no desire to build a relationship with. First impressions are not always correct in assessing whether a long-term connection will develop from the first meeting, as I have developed authentic relationships with people I initially did not trust.

Business and social psychology are beginning to intertwine in the new Relationship Era:

> *Emotional intelligence is a term that is beginning to weave its way into M.B.A. studies and business planning. Emotional intelligence describes the ability, capacity, skill, or self-perceived ability to identify, assess, and manage the emotions of oneself, others, and groups. People who possess a high degree of emotional intelligence know themselves very well and can also sense the emotions of others. They are affable, resilient, and optimistic. Surprisingly, emotional intelligence is a relatively recent behavioral model: it was not until the publication of* Emotional Intelligence: Why It Can Matter More Than IQ *by Goleman (1995) that the term became popular.*[10]

Research in emotional intelligence shows us that being honest and vulnerable is crucial to developing successful relationships in the business context.

Vulnerability means exposing oneself emotionally in an uncertain environment. Brene Brown, the author of the best-selling book *Daring Greatly* and a professor at the University of Houston, mentioned in her well-known TED talk that "[w]e can embrace vulnerability that allows us to experience true authenticity, and thus true freedom and power in life."[11]

Establishing authentic relationships in business is not just a feel-good trend. Authentic relationships enable people to connect personally with you and your business, which leads to a more fruitful relationship. Developing a more profound relationship means that you are seeking to understand what motivates a person. When you get to know someone personally, you will better understand what motivates them professionally. Developing a relationship professionally will encourage your prospects and clients to understand you and become your ambassadors. It brings a level of substance to your services that elevate your business above the competition. Your brand is identified as influential, reliable, and trustworthy.

As the business world trends to more virtual interaction, we see a growing realization and hunger for genuine relationships. Your intention in starting an authentic relationship is vital. Is it transactional (what can I get out of this relationship), or is it relational (will this trusted relationship benefit each other)? Your mindset needs to be one of a genuine desire to be of service and value to others.

Michael

I first met Michael at a networking event at a downtown bank. He was a successful vice president at a large insurance agency in Seattle. He was dressed in his finest suit with slicked-back hair. He was amiable and charismatic. My first impression was, here is a New York Godfather-looking salesperson. Probably not a good fit values-wise for developing a relationship with him. Boy, did I get that wrong.

The majority of my clients have come from expanding my network and building relationships with key individuals. One individual, a banker, introduced me to a prospective client whose business she was helping to finance. I was one of three CFOs that the prospective client was introduced to. Once an introduction is made, it is up to me to connect with the prospective client and determine if it is a good fit. This client took a week to contact the three CFOs and then welcomed me to the team. I have now worked with this client the longest of all my clients.

I have found that when there is an alliance in values, the decision to move forward in a partnership is a slam dunk. There is no competition. An alliance of values also allows for an authentic relationship to develop. My client can call me anytime and rant or worry or celebrate, and I am there for him. I can encourage him with good news and be honest with him with challenging information. I have had lunch in his home and gone fishing with him on a lake by his house. We talked about family, sports, and politics. We are in business together.

A significant factor in growing my successful CFO practice has been expanding my network. For many people, this can be an intimidating and tiring experience. There were times where I asked myself if I wanted to meet another banker, real estate agent, financial planner, or insurance agent. How can I possibly decide who I need to spend more time developing a relationship with? If one of my clients needs a banker or insurance agent, who do I introduce them to?

Michael followed up with me, and we met for coffee. He also joined a networking group that I was a member of, and I got to know him even better. Michael was super-friendly and was always asking what he could do for me. His authentic self and personality began to break down the barriers I had erected.

I began to meet with him and his wife regarding a new concept for an insurance agency that they were working on. They invited me to join them with my wife at a happy hour. Lunches and dinners followed as they became genuine friends. Michael also did CEO consulting along with his insurance practice and began to talk about several of his clients that he was thinking about bringing me in on as a CFO. Eventually, he introduced me to a fast-growing business owner that had grown to a level of needing a consulting CFO. This client has now become my second-largest client.

How do you know you have picked the right person to build a relationship with? For me, I had to look past my biases and see the real person who aligned with my values. Michael and I continue to work with our joint client. Oh, and as a bonus, Michael's mom is a travel agent, and they put together a screaming deal for a river cruise in Europe that we were invited to join them on. This cruise resulted in a lifetime of memories. And who thought networking could be so rewarding?

Evidence Of Authentic Relationships

Business is all about relationships, how well you build them determines how well they build your business.[12]

—BRAD SUGARS, BUSINESS AND WEALTH COACH

Developing authentic relationships is a long-term strategy. When a connection is formed and matured with the right people, the return on that investment will far exceed the value of focusing on one-time transactions. Long-term relationships are nurtured over the years. The financial benefit comes from providing a service or product that is truly needed and desired by your customer and not based on a perceived need.

Building authentic relationships in business is not necessarily easy. It does take patience and a focus on relationships over transactions. Traditionally success is measured by how many deals are closed. The metrics of this new Relationship Era should measure success by the number of authentic relationships developed and nurtured. The immediate impact of developing authentic relationships may not be evident, but genuine relationships will result in a stronger and more profitable business in the long term.

Eighty-five percent of executives surveyed agree that in-person meetings build stronger, more meaningful business relationships.[13] Face-to-face meetings allow for better interactions between participants. The ability to "read" emotions and reactions is essential in developing a relationship that serves both parties. The meeting will be more memorable and have a better chance of a lasting impact than a virtual meeting. There are many good reasons to meet virtually in business. It can be very efficient and save time and money. However, if your goal is to develop authentic relationships, in-person is your best option.

Another way to develop a strong connection with someone is to ask questions. Curiosity about what a person is thinking and feeling helps build a positive emotional connection. Neuroscience research shows that our brain actively engages in two different domains: an analytical domain, which is task-focused, and an empathic domain, which is relational.[14] Empathy is crucial for successful social interactions, as it allows one to predict someone else's actions, intentions, and emotions. Questions that focus on building positive emotion activate the empathic domain. When the empathic domain is activated, we are more open to understanding and relating to the person we speak to. Empathy builds more robust connections and deeper relationships.

Have you noticed that your brain is constantly generating thoughts about the environment we are in, including the thoughts about the conversation we are having? Our brain tends to keep a continual commentary going about people we meet and what they are saying. This commentary includes labeling people in a good or bad way. This commentary tends to be cautious or skeptical when it comes to developing relationships. It is essential to be aware of what our brains are doing and understand that the commentary may be based on experience and not based on the current interaction. Recognizing that our brains have the limitation of focusing on our past experiences and not allowing the negative chatter to stand in the way of developing an authentic relationship is a powerful way to engage emotional intelligence positively.

This chatter in our brains, when someone is talking, causes us to pay only partial attention to what the other person is saying. The commentary in our brains starts thinking about how we will respond or what we think about what the person is saying. Emotional intelligence recognizes this commentary and forces the brain to pay close attention to the words that are being said without thinking of a response or judgment on what is being said. A relationship begins to develop when we listen carefully and pay attention to the person's emotions and body language. Empathy helps us feel what the other person is feeling. When empathy and understanding are reflected back to the speaker, they feel understood and valued. This is the start of developing an authentic relationship.

A willingness to be vulnerable in a relationship will help build a stronger connection as well. We all have personal experiences and thoughts that are not shared widely. When you sense that the person you are talking with may be judgmental in nature or might not hold a conversation in confidence, you will be less likely to share your thoughts. Because there is risk in sharing your dreams of the future or a meaningful experience, trust is essential for any relationship to develop. When we share something of a personal nature, we send a signal to the other person that we trust them. This will then lead that person to become more open with you and feel worthy of your trust. It all starts with being willing to be vulnerable.

Authenticity and trust in relationships make a critical foundation for high-performing business teams. In her book *Love 2.0*, Barbara Frederickson dives even deeper into the benefits of human connection and relationships, and demonstrates that love resides in connections. Our Western culture would relegate emotions of love for private or romantic events. Fredrickson suggests, "Love is a momentary upwelling of three tightly interwoven events:

first, a sharing of one or more positive emotions between you and another; second, a synchrony between your and the other person's biochemistry and behaviors; and third, a reflected motive to invest in each other's well-being that brings mutual care."[15] The thought of calling authentic relationships a representation of love will cause a great deal of unease in the business world. Based on Fredrickson's definition, however, love is about mutual care. This is a quality that should be evident in every business.

Authentic relationships are not transactional. A transactional relationship would focus on what I can get out of this relationship and transaction. A genuine relationship considers the opposite of what is in it for me, but rather what I am able to do that will benefit you. A mutual relationship of care focuses on the beneficial rewards to both parties. People in genuine relationships respond consistently to each other regardless of the situation.

Genuine relationships become personal. If the desire is to invest in the other person's well-being, you seek to understand what drives and motivates them outside of the business context. What are they passionate about? What values encourage them to do what they do? What common areas of interest do you have with them? The more you can understand all aspects of the other person, the better you will understand what motivates them professionally.

Developing authentic relationships has multiple benefits for your business and the rest of your life. It might not always show up in the form of money but could lead to your personal growth or opportunities outside of the business. Investing in authentic relationships with your time, resources, connections, and expertise will lead to a richer and more rewarding life and business.

How You Can Develop More Authentic Relationships

Developing and maintaining authentic relationships takes intentionality and focus. Each point below is not difficult to do but is quite easy not to do.

1. Look to serve before you are served. What can you do to provide value to the other person? Put your own needs and wants on hold as you develop the relationship.

2. Do not allow fear to prevent you from taking action. Fear of being taken advantage of or rejected will cause you to miss out on the potential to create deep relationships.

3. Approach relationships with boldness. Live, speak, and act with courage, passion, and truth.

4. Be your authentic self. This may go without saying, but if you want to have genuine relationships, you need to be authentic in your passion and mission every moment of the day.

5. Consistency is critical in developing long-term relationships. When a person experiences the consistent message that you care about their well-being, trust and understanding naturally develop.

6. Always be willing to take responsibility for your mistakes. Authenticity means being transparent.

7. Be accountable for what you promise. If you tell someone you are going to do something for them, be sure to follow through.

8. Developing authentic relationships take time and attention. Give your full attention to the people you are talking with. Be willing to share your knowledge and expertise for their benefit, not your own.

The real power of authenticity can be uncomfortable and scary at times. Embracing the value of authentic relationships in business will always inspire others and bring value to all involved. This is the future of business.

CHAPTER 4

Operating in Integrity

> *The glue that holds all relationships together —*
> *including the relationship between the leader and the*
> *led is trust, and trust is based on integrity.*
>
> —BRYAN TRACY

What Is Integrity?

The business world has many stories of business owners who skirt the rules: salespeople who tell their prospects what they want to hear, knowing they will never be able to fulfill their promises, and human resource people who look at employees as an asset but tell them they appreciate them as people.

What is integrity? Integrity is defined as: "The quality of being honest and having strong moral principles."[16]

Integrity means doing the right thing because it is the right thing to do. Integrity means always to tell the truth. Integrity is a state of mind. Integrity always errs on the side of fairness. The word comes from the Latin word "integer," which stands for untouched, pure, honest, and sound. When you act with integrity, you present yourself as the same person to different people and different scenarios. Integrity is doing what you say even when there is no one there to see you doing it.

> *It is impossible for us to proceed in any kind of a relationship unless we trust and feel confident with the other person.*[17]
>
> —BRIAN TRACY

Integrity: A Deeper Look

The key to acting with integrity is to understand what your values are and then to be true to those values. It comes down to honesty.

There are many stories in society and businesses of people who struggle with making an ethical decision when faced with intense pressure to act in a way that is unethical. Having a code of ethics isn't going to stop unethical behavior, just as having laws isn't going to stop crime. Each person needs to internalize their code of ethics and choose in advance to operate according to this code so that when a difficult situation arises, the first response is to act according to a pre-established set of ethics. Decisions may have to be made that involve a choice between the lesser of two evils. A simple code of ethics isn't going to address complex situations directly, and so something more is needed for a person to feel confident in making difficult ethical decisions.

Conflicts will arise between a company and its community any time profits are pursued. The resolutions to these conflicts do not always come easily. People are often conflicted with balancing the pursuit of the "good life" with what is right for society.

There is an underlying sense among many businesspeople that when operating in a highly competitive environment, the only way to "win" is to be less than truthful or compassionate in their business dealings. Indeed, in the short term, this may very well be true. The competition may operate from rules that are less than virtuous and will be able to gain access to contracts and customers that a more virtuous and honest company would lose out on. The other side of this argument is that in the long term, an open, honest, and compassionate company will have an advantage over a less honest company. There is no guarantee that a company that operates from a strict Judeo-Christian ethic will necessarily have the same success as a company that doesn't follow this code of ethics.

> *Trust is like the air we breathe—when it's present, nobody really notices. When it's absent, everyone notices.*[18]
> —WARREN BUFFETT

A Story Of Integrity

My W-2 career in accounting and finance has, on occasion, challenged my ability to live up to my value of integrity. At one company where I worked, it was clear early on that my values didn't match the owners' or the VP of Operation's values.

I was the Controller in this company, and part of my duties included handling the human resource functions. One day, officials from Immigration and Naturalization Service came into the office to audit the I-9 forms. My records were all in place and accurately filled out. However, many of these forms contained fake Social Security numbers. I had physically viewed each document, and they looked legitimate to me, so I had done my job. The workers with fake Social Security numbers were escorted off of the premises.

It only took a couple of days, and the same workers started being rehired with new Social Security numbers. I was told by Larry, the VP of Operations, to sign the I-9 forms without question. I knew Larry had a temper and was known to yell and intimidate to get his way. Technically I could have signed the I-9s because the Social Security cards looked legitimate. However, I knew these were the same people that had been escorted off of the premises a few days earlier. I told Larry that I would not sign the forms. I could see the anger rising in Larry. There was a tense moment where I thought I might be fired on the spot. He had the power to do that. Finally, Larry said he would sign the forms himself and stormed out of my office.

To this day, I am glad I did not go against my value of integrity. I believe that, had I signed the forms, I would have forever regretted the decision.

My CFO Business Partner practice is built on a monthly recurring billing basis where each client understands the value that they will receive each month. My promise to each client is if they do not believe that they have received as much value as what I am billing that I will reduce my billing to match their perceived value. I have never been asked by a client to reduce my billing. However, I evaluate my work each month and ask myself if I have provided the value that I have promised.

One client, in particular, has been challenging for a number of reasons. The outsourced bookkeeper retired from her practice, and my client struggled to find a replacement that could live up to the owner's spouse's expectations. I offered to provide a bookkeeper through my practice, but the spouse thought she could handle the bookkeeping herself and didn't want to spend the extra money. The result has been slow invoicing, slow collections, not entering bills into QuickBooks, and no bank reconciliations. I could go on. With inadequate and delayed records, my financial analysis was of little value.

I told the owner about the challenges and that I was not a bookkeeper. I would do what needed to be done to make sure transactions were recorded each month, but nothing else. My analysis of the value I was providing pointed out that my billing was too high. I reduced my billing amount without being asked. I could easily have continued billing the same amount. I also could have just quit working with this client and would have been justified. Neither of these options felt like they would support my claim of working with integrity. I continue to work with this client. The goal is to find a buyer for the company and allow the owner to move into a consulting position to continue to do what he loves to do without the complications of accounting for what is happening. This will be a win for both of us if we can get that accomplished.

Evidence Of Integrity

Integrity is the most valuable and respected quality of leadership. Always keep your word.[19]

—BRIAN TRACY

Brian Tracy has written and spoken many times about leadership and integrity. In his blog, Tracy outlines many key aspects of how leaders must lead with integrity.

Recognized and respected leaders keep their promises. They are careful to make promises, wanting to make sure that if they give their word on something, it can be carried out. Once they make a promise, they do everything in their power to follow through on the promises they have made. They are also known to always tell the truth. Jack Welch calls it "candor." If a leader is afraid of being candid, then they will likely not be an effective leader.[20]

Leaders with integrity are not afraid to face the truth. This is called the reality principle, or "seeing the world as it really is, not as you wish it to be." It is perhaps the most important principle of leadership and dependent on integrity because it demands truthfulness and honesty. Many companies and organizations fail because they don't follow the reality principle. Integrity means telling the truth even if the truth is ugly. Better to be honest than to delude others, because then you are probably deluding yourself, too.

Leaders need to be courageous, but they also need to be open to the idea that they could be wrong. There are many leaders who eventually fail because they refuse to question their own assumptions or conclusions.

> *Errant assumptions lie at the root of every failure.*[21]
> —ALEC MACKENZIE

There's a difference between being confident and blind. Let's face it, in today's world of rapid change, there is a possibility that you are partially wrong or even completely wrong. Maybe you are not wrong, but just opening yourself up to that possibility will make you a more effective leader because it will open your mind to new ideas or new thinking.

There should be no exceptions to honesty and integrity. Integrity is a state of mind and is not situational. If you compromise your integrity in small situations with little consequence, it becomes very easy to compromise on larger cases. Leaders with integrity always err on the side of fairness, especially when other people are unfair. The true mark of leadership is how fair you can be when other people are mistreating you.

Leadership matters in setting the direction of a corporation, but it is also critical that the top leaders set an example from an integrity and ethical perspective. The leader of a company must be transparent about its operations. Each decision that is made should be able to stand up to public scrutiny. There will always be detractors, but with adequate explanation, a decision should be able to make sense to the average worker of the company.

A leader operating with integrity should consider the company as an active part of the community. When the leader looks at the community as more than just an economic market, as well as being an active citizen that is interested in the well-being of the community, good things happen. They should represent their products honestly and be proactive in caring for their customer. This customer care goes beyond just delivering a product and collecting a check.

Finally, integrity would demand that a leader values and treats their employees as a partner and team member in the business's success. The principle-centered leader focuses on helping others succeed and bringing out the most in the people who are being led. Stephen Covey, in his book *Principle-Centered Leadership*, points to this when he said:

Principle-centered leadership suggests that the highest level of human motivation is a sense of personal contribution. It views people as the most valuable organizational assets — as stewards of specific resources — and stewardship as the key to discovering, developing, and managing all other assets. Each person is recognized as a free agent capable of immense achievement, not a victim or pawn limited by conditions or conditioning.[22]

Integrity in business is an essential ingredient for sustainable, long-term business growth, and success. It can be hard to define and difficult to measure, but you know it when you see it, and it's clear when it's not there. It's evident that acting with integrity can be hard to do; it's equally apparent that we all want to be treated that way by others. Leaders with integrity may not be the most famous or flashy of leaders, and they don't care. Integrity means doing the right thing because it is the right thing to do. And that is how success should be measured.

APPLICATION

How Can You Develop More Integrity?

There are several things to keep in mind as you navigate the business world with integrity. First is an acknowledgment that our laws are based on an ethics of right and wrong. Second, industry or company codes of ethics are important to follow. Third, almost all humans have a general sense of right and wrong, or a moral compass and, and this should be followed. Fourth, obey the golden rule: do unto others what you would have them do to you. Fifth, if you don't want the public to see what you are doing, don't do it. Sixth, do no harm to others that would be considered irresponsible.

The following may not seem related to integrity, but I have found that a person of integrity has many of the following characteristics:

1. They are continually learning and working on improving themselves.

2. They are service-oriented, always looking to help others.

3. They radiate positive energy and a can-do attitude.

4. They believe in other people and willingly invest themselves in others.

5. They lead balanced lives. They realize that there is more to life than just making money.

6. They look at life as an adventure and make the most of it.

Do you see yourself in these characteristics? If not, consider ways to focus on never-ending improvement.

CHAPTER 5

Follow Extraordinary Stewardship

What Is Stewardship?

The term "stewardship" has multiple meanings in various contexts. Still, the following fits the business context well: the conducting, supervising, or managing of something, *and* the careful and responsible management of something entrusted to one's care.

Stewardship is about service to something greater. It requires a redistribution of power and privilege, moving choice and resources closer to the organizations' edges. Stewardship asks us to be deeply accountable for our organization's outcomes without trying to control others or trying to take care of them.

Peter Block approaches the issue of leadership in the face of the changing environment of business from a stewardship perspective. His primary thesis is that the focus on individual leaders as the critical agent for meeting the new marketplace's challenges is misplaced. Instead, he believes that "it is this pervasive and almost religious belief in leaders that slows the process of genuine reform."[23] On the other hand, empowerment is the belief that the answer to many of the problematic questions of business lies within each person working for an organization. Stewardship then becomes an issue of giving away power to those who may have the least "important" position in a company to make decisions. Block drives to the heart of the issue by saying:

> *Stewardship begins with the willingness to be accountable for a larger body than ourselves – an organization, a community. Stewardship springs from a set of beliefs about reforming organizations that affirms our choice for service over the pursuit of self-interest. When we choose service over self-interest, we say we are willing to be deeply accountable without controlling the world around us.*[24]

Stewardship: A Deeper Look

Prioritizing service over self-interest runs entirely counter to the way most business leaders have been trained. The idea that leaders would willingly put themselves in a position that would require them to be held accountable for an action or decision that is entirely outside of their control is unlikely. And yet, I see this as a critical part of creating an environment of extraordinary business stewardship. Trusting and believing that every person is created to make decisions and will, if given the opportunity, make decisions that benefit the community or organization over self, lays the foundation for a transformational stewardship environment.

The business world has focused much of its time and resources on developing a business model that demands the largest monetary return on investment as possible. In result, shareholders and executive leaders of large, publicly held businesses have experienced incredible growth in wealth over the past few decades. However, this single focus on monetary return has produced an ever-growing culture of greed and malfeasance with the likes of Enron, WorldCom, Tyco, Global Crossing, Wells Fargo, Volkswagen, Valeant Pharmaceutical, and the list goes on.

Simultaneous to this growth in wealth, the income or wealth gap continues to grow, with the majority of the nation's wealth under the control of those responsible for leading businesses. Before President Obama's 2014 State of the Union Address, the media reported that the top wealthiest 1 percent possess 40 percent of the nation's wealth; the bottom 80 percent own 7 percent.[25] More recently, the media reported the "richest 1 percent in the United States now own more wealth than the bottom 90 percent."[26] The gap between the top 10 percent, and the middle class is over 1,000 percent; that increases another 1,000 percent for the top 1 percent. The average employee "needs to work more than a month to earn what the CEO makes in one hour."[27]

The traditional business approach focuses on scale and speed, reducing costs, getting bigger, and beating the competitors. Business is approached as a zero-sum game in many cases, meaning either you win or the competition wins. There is no consideration of creating a win-win environment. The concept of win-lose is undoubtedly true in gambling; however, in business, an environment should be set up in which a company is profitable, people will be developed, partners are treated fairly, and the community can flourish.

Corporate and small business America would be wise to begin looking beyond attaining as high a net profit as possible. They should start seeking ways to help their people develop to their best potential, operating with integrity and fairness with vendors and customers, and working towards helping their communities prosper. Extraordinary stewardship in business is a company that generates a reasonable profit, develops the people who work for it, treats clients and vendors with respect, and is proactive in investing back into the community. This stewardship creates a healthy ecosystem in which all may grow and thrive.

The Story Of Stewardship

The COVID-19 pandemic has created multiple challenges for businesses and our economy in general. When the order to shut down non-essential companies came down from the Governor of Washington, there was a scramble to figure out what businesses were essential. Most of my clients were deemed essential services and continued to operate. However, that did not ease the anxiety of how a collapsing economy would affect business. When the federal government introduced the Paycheck Protection Program (PPP) through the Small Business Administration, there was an overall sense of relief to have a source of funds in the event the virus and economy worsened.

A1 Pallets was one such company, founded and owned by Amrik. We determined that it was an essential business because it supplied pallets to the essential transportation industry. Amrik's business has grown steadily over the past few years and was producing a substantial cash balance. The company had also incurred debt to automate the pallet manufacturing process. Business remained strong as the pandemic spread throughout the country. It appeared as though the business would come out relatively unscathed through this national emergency.

The decision to apply for the PPP loan was being made as the cash balance remained steady, revenue remained constant, and the business's future was looking strong. Should we apply for the loan? We were relatively confident we would be able to have the full loan forgiven through the forgiveness program, and so this was, in essence, "free" money. Could we make an argument that we were sufficiently concerned about how COVID-19 might yet impact the company? We decided that we met the qualifications for the loan and proceeded to fill out the applications. Amrik's enterprise was made up of three separate businesses with employees, so applications were submitted for all three businesses.

The question may come to the reader's mind as to how this relates to stewardship. As I was advising Amrik about the PPP loan, I was filtering my advice through the lens of stewardship. First, there was no guarantee that the virus would not impact the business in the future. If the economy turned to a recession due to the virus, it would be prudent and good stewardship to build up additional reserves to face a potentially severe recession. Second, we qualified for the loans, and it was reasonable to take advantage of a government program that we qualified for and would assure that personnel pay would not be cut. Third, I told Amrik that, if at the end of the virus and the lingering effects, it was clear that we did not need the extra funds, that he should consider contributing the funds to his family foundation. This foundation was started to help fund a hospital building in the small village in India where Amrik grew up.

Filtering the decision through the matrix of stewarding profits, people, partners, and places, it became an easy decision that matched my values well.

Evidence Of Stewardship

Many of us are familiar with the phrase "the triple bottom line" (TBL). This phrase was first coined in 1994 by John Elkington, the founder of a British consultancy called SustainAbility. He argued that companies should be preparing three different (and entirely separate) bottom lines. The TBL consists of three Ps: profit, people, and the planet. I would add a fourth P for partner, representing customers and vendors. TBL aims to measure the corporation's financial, social, and environmental performance over a set period. In the view of many, focusing attention on all three of these areas creates a sustainable business: a company that makes profits for its shareholders while protecting the environment and improving the lives of those with whom it interacts. It operates in such a way that business, environmental, and societal interests all intersect.

The foundation for building a sustainable business is to make a profit. But how much profit is necessary to sustain a business? How much of that profit should be invested back into the business? How much of the profit should go into the business owner's pocket? Good stewardship of profits carefully plans the answer to each of these questions. Long-term sustainability of the business depends on achieving the proper balance of stewarding the business's earnings.

I'm frequently called in to resolve a crisis caused by low-growth planning. Business explodes, yet the business is struggling with inadequate cash reserves. There's a demand for their product; however, the cash bottleneck is killing the company before selling the product. It is important for a business to steward profits and cash, so the cash shortages that growth often produces are built into their expansion strategy. Business growth is seldom a smooth ride. There are ups and downs, growth, and slowing. Stewardship demands that cash flow pinches are recognized and planned for.

A primary factor in most businesses' success is the people who work for the business. Caring for the people who work for the business by investing in their education, training, compensation, motivation, and empowerment creates a culture and environment that people want to give their best to the company with long-term employment. Stewarding people is a formula to create the environment to allow a company to flourish.

A good steward of people in business recognizes the importance of encouraging time off for employees. They realize that creating an environment of work-life balance increases productivity and creativity. This begins with the leader's attitude toward maintaining balance in life. The swells of failing to prioritize relationships and health will have an effect on business—often negatively. Karen Sumberg, Vice President and Director of Projects and Communications at the Center for Work-Life Policy, says, "You get tremendous burnout where people are not working at their full potential, they're not excited anymore, they're just perpetually tired."[28] That's not good for business.

Traditional business training suggests that a successful business is built by getting the most money from the customer and paying the least amount of money to the vendors. Stewarding partners would mean understanding the value of building loyalty with your customers and vendors by helping them flourish as well.

Stewarding your customers may mean not charging your customer the maximum price, or perhaps giving extended credit terms. Invest in developing expertise. Your customer's perception of what superior customer service looks like is best understood when you take the time to know your customer. Awesome customer service springs from a foundation of truly understanding your product or service and your customer. Using this knowledge to craft an experience for your customer that's targeted and feels personal is an investment toward achieving recognition for incredibly excellent customer service.

For the vendor, it may mean paying the bill faster than when it is due, or not buying from the cheapest supplier. When a vendor relationship begins, it is easy to focus on what the vendor will do for you. However, if the ongoing connection is only about you, partnerships will fail to form. Without the sense you have a vested interest in their success, most vendors just do the expected. Nothing motivates them to look for exceptional ways to help your business. Become a value creator. Becoming a successful steward of partners begins with you. Building loyalty through stewardship is an excellent insurance policy.

Every business is part of the community that surrounds it. In many ways, it is the community that supports the business endeavor. It is vital for a business to steward this relationship with the community in a way that allows the community to flourish. Healthy communities foster a healthy business environment. Small businesses need to work in partnership with each other and their communities to gain an economy of scale and influence to compete with larger corporations. There is power in unity and the collective efforts of business and community. So much more can be accomplished in the community when stewardship of place focuses on the business community. Supporting the civic, education, nonprofit, and faith sectors of the community is also good for business.

APPLICATION

Stewardship is great in theory, but what are some practical ways a business owner or leader can implement this strategy? How can a traditional numbers kind of CFO start to think about a business like a CSO (Chief Stewardship Officer)?

1. Stewarding profits means identifying what net profit is adequate to provide a reasonable return for the owner's investment and not distributing more than this amount to the owner.

2. Stewarding profits means determining how much working capital is necessary for a business to operate safely and invest the rest into personnel and the community.

3. Stewarding people means treating personnel as partners in the business and not as a resource or asset.

4. Stewarding people means investing in personnel to help them become better workers, parents, spouses, and community leaders.

5. Stewarding partners means helping customers and vendors become successful in their businesses.

6. Stewarding partners means developing relationships with customers and vendors, and understanding what is important to them.

7. Stewarding places means investing in the community in ways that allow the community to flourish.

8. Stewarding places means understanding the community is as crucial to your business success as you are.

CHAPTER 6

Pursue An Attitude Of Service

The guru of servant-leadership is Robert Greenleaf. He stated that the primary guide for a leader pursuing an attitude of service "begins with the natural feeling that one wants to serve, to serve first. Then conscious choice brings one to aspire to lead."[29]

What Is An Attitude Of Service?

The concept of leading in business with an attitude of service generally runs counter to what most management and leadership books have taught in the past. The qualities associated with strong leadership and sound management in an organization seldom include an attitude of service. And yet many people believe that servant-leadership is the right thing to do.

Pursuing An Attitude Of Service: A Deeper Look

The servant-leader is the person who has a natural desire to put others' interests before their own. They are driven by the desire to see others grow and develop as people and workers to their greatest potential. They are willing to put aside their own goals to help others accomplish their purposes. They live a life of integrity where what they say is what they do, both at work and at home.

Other characteristics that describe a servant-leader are listening, empathy, awareness, foresight, stewardship, community, and a commitment to people's growth. The organization that is led by a servant-leader will have staff that is confident in their abilities. They will likely reflect the servant-leader's action by being willing to serve others as well. They will be known for their high customer service level and likely be a place where others will want to work because of their reputation of kindness.

James Sipe and Don Frick expand on Robert Greenleaf's definition of a servant-leader in their book. Sipe and Frick define a servant-leader as "a person of character, who puts people first. He or she is a skilled communicator, a compassionate collaborator who has foresight, is a systems thinker, and leads with moral authority."[30]

One of the servant-leader's primary qualities is the evidence of love for others. Love in the workplace is demonstrated by patience, kindness, humbleness, respect, selflessness, forgiveness, honesty, and commitment. Living out these qualities of love in the workplace will set a person apart in most organizations.

The Story Of An Attitude Of Service

I have been putting together budgets for different businesses and organizations for over thirty-five years. I have been involved in several other processes as I have put these budgets together. My budget role for smaller non-profit organizations was to look at historical income and expenses, understand whether the organization was growing or not, and project out estimated numbers based on this data. There was seldom input from other board members or administrators because they were not skilled in this area and trusted me to do a good job. I could explain why I chose different income and expense numbers, and that usually satisfied everyone. My budget role with larger for-profit businesses was similar to the above. Still, the owner generally had an idea of the amount of profit he wanted to generate, and I had to build a budget that fits that profit goal. Again, I seldom had input from the people involved in sales and operations, other than telling them this is your budget.

One of the organizations that I worked for, Bakke Graduate University (BGU), indicated a desire to have as many people provide input into the budget process as possible. Based on this input, it was decided to use extended staff time to work on budget preparation. I was somewhat reluctant to leave the entire process to the staff's mercy, but the process felt like it fit the school's philosophy of "Joy at Work." It dawned on me that I had never applied the concept of servant-leadership to a budget process. I decided that this would be an excellent opportunity to design this approach into the budget preparation process.

As I considered how to incorporate servant-leadership into the budgeting process, I needed to develop a vision of why this would be an essential design process. Andy Stanley states, "Vision weaves four things into the fabric of our daily experience. 1) Passion. Vision evokes emotion. 2) Motivation. Vision provides motivation. 3) Direction. Vision sets a direction. 4) Purpose. Vision translates into purpose." [31]

One of my passions is to create a detailed budget and watch over the year to see how close my numbers line up with the actual numbers. If I could share that passion and create joy for the staff in the process of budgeting, then much of what I was aiming to accomplish would be achieved. My motivation is to know that if I do an excellent job of projecting future income and expenses, the organization's planning can be much more effective. The direction I wanted to set was to engage the staff in owning the final budget numbers and providing them with an education about the process and understanding what areas of the school affect each part of the budget. Ken Blanchard and Phil Hodges say, "Another key element of being a servant-leader is to consider people's development as an equal end goal as their performance." [32]

This then leads to the purpose of setting aside time to work together on a budget. With this backdrop, I proceeded to launch the BGU budget process with an attitude of service. As I mentioned earlier, I have always enjoyed putting together budgets and watching how close my projections come to the actual numbers. This process of team collaboration and input was a new experience for me. The challenge in using the team approach is that it takes longer to coach and train other people than to just do it myself. However, the upside to this process is I can build deeper relationships with the staff. I am also able to build loyalty and trust. By asking for input and trusting the team to do the hard work of deciding on different projections, a sense of camaraderie developed. Staff now also have a deeper understanding of how we arrive at budget numbers and what sort of transactions and decisions affect the final budget numbers.

I end with an email I received from Professor of Pastoral Studies, Dr. Lowell Bakke:

> *Art,*
>
> *Thank you for this incredible amount of work you put into the budget and the wonderfully transparent manner in which you did our part of the work. I reflect two or three years ago when we all wondered if we would make it physically and fiscally through the budget process. Pain, doubt, and even suspicion, were everywhere. Although I was in Boulder when most of the input was given you this*

year, I heard from so many how valuable and meaningful the process was to all the people involved. Thank you for setting the tone that gave both hope and honest reality to those involved. I realize the process is not over and that absolutely anything can happen in the days ahead to challenge the school. Still, please know that what has already been done is a profound blessing to us and an incredible example of why business and theology can and should be together. It is a beautiful model.

Blessings, Lowell.

Evidence Of Pursuing An Attitude Of Service

> *Organizations exist to serve. Period.*
> *Leaders live to serve. Period.*[33]
> —TOM PETERS

Many executives in business would disagree with Peters' understanding of leadership. Many people who are in positions of power would look at "servanthood" as a weakness. They see this type of leadership as beneath their dignity and putting themselves in a position to be taken advantage of.

Simon Sinek has worked with organizations around the world. He has observed team environments that generate deep trust with each other. They are high functioning teams that foster trust and are willing to do whatever it takes to help their team members. Other groups are dysfunctional, fragmented, and on the verge of failure. These teams are driven by cynicism, paranoia, and self-interest. What is the critical difference between these two types of groups? In most cases it comes down to leadership.

In his book *Leaders Eat Last*, Simon Sinek describes what he calls a "Circle of Safety" as the catalyst to foster trust and cooperation inside teams.[34] This circle of safety protects the security of the team from the challenges of outside forces. The group focuses on helping each other inside the team succeed rather than taking individual credit to make management happy. The concept is that when we get to know each other and trust that each person within the team has your back, then we are more likely to freely exchange information and ideas that will benefit the organization and move it forward. Without trust, the team members will be afraid information that they share will be used against them. Or someone else will take credit for a new innovative idea. When a leader provides a safe environment for the team to work, they will put their best efforts forward. A servant-leader creates a work environment of encouragement. Workers in an environment of encouragement are free to learn, feel valued, and thrive. Productivity soars and people flourish. A synergy is developed and collaboration increases.

Servant-leadership in business is not just a theory in academia. The following are seven large companies that have made leading by serving an essential foundation for success:[35]

FedEx was founded in 1971 by Fred Smith, who still leads the company as CEO. He believes "when people are placed first, they will provide the highest possible service, and profits will follow." What emerged from this thinking is a distinctive company culture. The "People-Service-Profit" philosophy has helped the company grow rapidly and remain competitive.

Marriott is another company founded on a "people first" philosophy. As another service company, the thinking is very similar: "Take care of associates, and they will take care of the customers."

Starbucks may not be an obvious choice of servant-leadership organization, but the culture of inclusion and social responsibility is deeply rooted in servant-leadership. Howard Schultz is described here as a true servant leader.

SAS is a leader in data analytics and artificial intelligence, based in North Carolina. SAS believes "in empowering our employees to change the way the world works." As Jim Goodnight, the founder and CEO, says, "Treat employees like they make a difference, and they will."

The Container Store is the leading specialty retailer of storage and organization products in the United States. The Container Store fosters an employee-first culture built around its Foundation Principles. These principles were formalized by Chairman Kip Tindell and all the employees of their Houston store when it first opened in 1988.

"At TDIndustries, we have a diverse, people-centered culture built on a foundation of trust. We accomplish this through a servant-leadership philosophy that puts others first."

Garry Ridge, the chairman and CEO of WD-40, believes that "Leadership is about learning and teaching." He co-authored a book called *Helping People Win at Work* with Ken Blanchard. He's also an advocate of Simon Sinek and the "'leaders eat last" mentality. At WD-40, he has successfully created a culture of servant-leadership based on the idea of the team as a tribe.

Pursuing an attitude of service is a characteristic of success for many businesses. They have a people-focused culture that ensures meaningful stability during times of rapid change. Many business thinkers and writers recognize the value of servant-leadership. The attitude is increasingly relevant to the challenges in today's business.

> *The key to greatness is to look for people's potential and spend time developing it.*[36]
>
> —PETER DRUCKER

APPLICATION

How can you pursue an attitude of service?

To help us recognize servant-leadership, Robert Greenleaf gave us a test for servant-leaders in business and servant-leadership organizations. He called it the Best Test:

1. Do those served grow as persons?

2. While being served, do they become healthier, wiser, freer, more autonomous, more likely themselves to become servants?

3. What is the effect on the least privileged in society?

4. Will they benefit or at least not be further deprived?[37]

To be an effective servant-leader, you must be honest and accountable for your actions. You should possess a high degree of emotional intelligence. You must be competent for the job at hand. Your attitude must be of one who is willing to learn and be coachable. This includes self-awareness about your strengths and weaknesses.

CHAPTER 7

Value The Individual

Roy E. Disney was a longtime senior executive for the Walt Disney Company, which was founded by his father, Roy Oliver Disney, and his uncle, Walt Disney.

As the last member of the Disney family to be actively involved in the company, Roy Disney was often compared to his uncle and father. In 2006, Forbes magazine estimated his personal fortune at $1.2 billion. He died in 2009.

During the late 1980s and 1990s, Roy Disney's department produced a number of commercially successful and critically acclaimed films. The era has been called a renaissance for the company and animation in general.

"It's not hard to make decisions, once you know what your values are," said Roy Disney.

What Does Valuing The Individual Look Like?

The fundamental importance of democracy is that each individual matters. No matter what walk of life a person comes from, each opinion and voice is unique. A business should treat every individual it interacts with, in a way that values their dignity and worth.

Today's workplace environment has had very little change in the past 250 years. Bureaucratic behavior remains the heart and soul of most work environments and managers have a tendency to treat workers like children unable to make good decisions and think for themselves. When a company values the individual employee the criteria for organizational performance and success is not measured primarily in financial terms, but rather that the workplace is filled with joy for the ordinary worker and is measured by the worker's quality of life.

As a business owner, I know you think about more than the revenue you generate. You also consider the costs your decisions will incur and the resulting margin you retain. Have you ever considered that the vendors you work with also have these concerns? If you want to build winning vendor relationships, it pays to communicate a strong message that you want to partner with your vendors. The message should be, "I want to help you grow and build a successful business as I grow mine." You want your clients to see you as a value creator, don't you? Consider the exponential value to you as a business if your vendors saw you in that light as well.

How do you deliver an incredibly awesome customer experience and know it's received by your clients as such? This is a question I ask myself as a consultant. It leads to asking additional questions of each customer. Your customer's perception of what superior customer service looks like is best understood when you take the time to know your customer.

Taking A Deeper Look At Valuing The Individual

Most businesses have employees to help operate and run their organization. Research suggests that many of these employees feel like just a cog in the wheel and underappreciated. The sentiment by many business owners is that employees are assets to be leveraged for greater profits. Dennis Bakke wrote the book *Joy at Work* to lay out the premise that the workplace should be fun and fulfilling. The average worker all around the world can experience the feelings of fulfillment and joy by giving him or her the ability to make important and critical business decisions. The worker whose job is most affected by a decision should be the one making the decision. When an organization values the individual, then this process must be not only embraced but supported to help the employee succeed.

A critical component of this decision needs to include input from co-workers and supervisors. If input is received and relied on, it doesn't matter if the decision turned out good or bad. Everyone will make mistakes occasionally; these are critical learning times for employees which will only strengthen the ability of that worker to make a better decision next time.

Another key aspect is to build in scorekeeping, accountability, and rewards. When decisions are made, the employee is held accountable for the outcome. The individual must admit when they make an error, ask forgiveness, and promise to try not make the same mistake again. Rewards and compensation must be fair and tied to performance.

The most important character traits of a leader are humility, the willingness to give up power, courage, integrity, love, and passion for people. This passion for people, valuing them as individuals, will also allow leaders to experience joy at work. Allowing the individual to have control and the decision-making authority gives all a chance to make their organization succeed.

Business owners think about more than the revenue they generate. They also consider the costs that are incurred when decisions are made and the resulting profit margins. When the value of the individual vendor is considered during this process, it is incumbent on the buyer to understand that the vendors will also have these profit concerns. This should result in conveying the message, "I want to help you grow and build a successful business as I grow mine." Consider the exponential value to you as a business if your vendors see you as a value-creator.

Creating a vision of the potential within each partnership begins with making sure you are as good a fit for your vendor as they are for you. Recognize the value of your vendor's time, especially when they are offering a service. Do your research so you have as lucid an understanding as possible of what your needs are. Then voice them clearly so your vendors know whether working with you will grow and build their businesses. Also, take some time to get to know what your vendor's needs are. What motivates their investment into their business? As you do this, you will identify partners who share complimentary philosophies in how they do business. This alignment complements your partnering fit.

When a vendor relationship begins, it is easy to focus on what the vendor is going to do for you. However, if the ongoing connection is only about you, partnerships will fail to form. Without the sense you have a vested interest in their success, most vendors just do the expected. Nothing motivates them to look for exceptional ways to help your business. Become a value creator. Becoming a successful partner begins with you valuing the vendor as an individual.

For many business owners, the customer holds a much greater value to the business simply because this is the business's source of revenue. However, the same principle holds true for treating customers as valued individuals as it does for vendors. Your customer's perception of what superior customer service looks like is best understood when you take the time to know your customer.

For many businesses, the speed with which you can resolve their customer service issues is mission-critical. Your excellent customer service could be your ability to implement a plan that blocks the onset of more mission crippling events than your competitor. You raise the bar for every business providing the same service. Customers may evaluate your customer service negatively if the time to reach a person is excessive or you can't solve their problem during their first call.

Invest in developing deep knowledge about your customer and expertise in your product. Really awesome customer service springs from a foundation of fully understanding your product, your customer and making sure they are a good match. Using this knowledge to craft an experience for your customer that is targeted and feels personal is an investment toward achieving recognition for incredibly awesome customer service.

Valuing The Individual Success Story

I ended my W-2 career at a small non-residential, international higher education university called Bakke Graduate University (BGU) as their CFO. BGU had mid-career students from around the world. Many of these students lived in developing countries with extremely low wages. BGU's business model was highly dependent on contributions to cover scholarship assistance for these students.

This business model worked well for a number of years because of several deep pocket donors and a healthy enrollment of full tuition paying students. Then the Great Recession of 2008 hit the world's economies. Many students from developed countries began to delay their studies, putting stress on the student tuition revenue stream. Students with scholarships continued their studies because they had been granted full-ride scholarships. Donations began to drop off as the recession deepened and affected more of the economy.

BGU began to live on large donations, but it was not always easy to predict when they were coming in. On several occasions it was obvious from my projections that we were not going to have enough money to cover payroll. I knew from our development team that some large donations were in the works, but the funds would not be in our bank for several weeks. I had a conversation with each employee and asked them if they were able to wait several weeks for their paycheck. I assured each person that if they needed their paycheck that week, I would find a way to make sure they were paid. For those who could wait, I assured them that they would be paid at some point, but I could not guarantee exactly when. It was important to me to honor each individual's need and create a plan based on the individual.

BGU survived this crisis, and we came out of it with a strong sense of loyalty because of the way the employees were treated as individuals. However, the recession was still having a major effect on the economy and our donations. We were notified that our largest donor was going to be cutting his annual contributions by half. This was a significant amount. Based on this news, I projected that we were simply not going to be able to continue to operate without an infusion of new money. It was decided that I would lead a reduced budget shutdown over the course of seven months so that as many students could graduate as possible. The president would lead an initiative to raise the money needed to continue to operate.

As a non-residential graduate program, the majority of the expenses of the university was payroll. My only option to be able to continue operations for another seven months was to cut payroll significantly. I knew what the number was that I needed to reduce payroll by, but because I valued the individual, I chose to go back to the employee to ask what they were able to do. This time was different. I could not promise that they would be paid back for any reductions in payroll that I made. I could not promise that they would have a job after seven months. And yet, because I had honored each individual in the past economic crisis, I was given the opportunity to make the same ask. Each person was asked at what level of payroll could they make their personal budgets work. I again assured them that if they said they could not reduce their payroll amount I would pay them their full paycheck. There would be no pressure to change their decision. Their decision would not be revealed to any other staff.

The end of the story? BGU was able to continue for another seven months and graduate a large class. A number of employees found other employment over those months for a successful transition without a major impact to their budget. And BGU? They continue to operate with a reduced-staff business model and are affecting the world in a positive way.

Evidence Of Valuing The Individual

The evidence is clear that employee engagement has a large impact on business performance. As the Gallup 2017 State of the Global Workplace Report states, "engaged employees produce better business outcomes than do other employees across industry, across company size and nationality, and in good economic times and bad." [38] Another poll conducted by Gallup has uncovered that out of the world's one billion full-time workers, only 15 percent of people are engaged at work. That means that an astronomical 85 percent of people are unhappy in their jobs.

These statistics would suggest that the majority of employees do not feel valued as individuals. One key area of dissatisfaction is the amount of time off an employee receives. "Whether employees are salaried or receive overtime pay, they can only function at peak for so long without serious time off," Karen Sumberg, Vice President and Director of Projects and Communications at the Center for Work-Life Policy, says. "You get tremendous burnout where people are not working at their full potential, they're not excited anymore, they're just perpetually tired."[39] That's not good for business. Some companies are turning to an unlimited time off policy. In most cases this does not actually change the amount of time people take off from work, but it gives the employees a level of freedom that keeps them engaged in their work. There are many other reasons that create job dissatisfaction. Ultimately, the more an employer values each individual employee, the more likely they will build a culture of people who enjoy working for the company.

Valuing vendors in a business also can have a major impact on business success. Change Factory, an Australian change management company, says it well: "Vendors hold a wealth of knowledge relating to their products or services. A vendor also holds knowledge on utilization within industry. That knowledge helps you, as a client, achieve your objectives."[40]

In a *Huffington Post* blog post, Renate Cunneen suggests that:

> *"...the biggest mistake clients make when dealing with outsourced vendors" is to bring vendors on board, and then to "not listen to them when they try to give us clear feedback on our own shop." Part of growth in human beings and in business is listening to what you may be missing in yourself that someone else can see from the outside. Growth is hearing what we don't really want to hear, accepting it, facing it, and making the real attempts [sic] to change it. Maybe there are cracks in your own business that the vendor can clearly see from the outside; why wouldn't you want this type of feedback? Above all, how many vendors will give you this feedback? Many won't if there is not a level of trust where they feel comfortable enough to share candid feedback. That in itself is a tragedy.[41]*

The business world measures customer value by determining whether the customer feels like they received enough value for the price they paid for the product or service. For many businesses, this is simply a dollars-and-sense determination. However, it is important to remember that customers respond positively to a number of tangible and intangible benefits. Some examples are how the product will help them achieve their goals, or how the product may make them feel. They also respond positively to feeling valued and appreciated as a customer.

Similarly, there are different types of benefits that influence customer decisions. Some examples include tangible benefits such as, how the product will help them achieve goals, as well as image benefits, such as, how owning this product or service will change one's social status in the eyes of their peers and colleagues.

There have been many studies comparing customer acquisition costs to customer retention costs. It is widely accepted that it costs five times as much to acquire a new customer then to retain an existing customer. Spending time and resources to make personal connections to customers and understanding their needs is money well spent.

APPLICATION

How Do I Show My Employees I Value Them?

► Give employees the authority and responsibility to make key decisions in areas that directly impact their work.

► Provide guilt-free time off for each employee.

► Show that you care by asking questions and getting to know each employee personally.

How Do I Show My Vendors That I Value Them?

► Focus on the value the partnership creates for both of you.

► Do the right thing. No vendor should suffer because of decisions we make.

► Have ongoing conversations with existing vendors to maintain the relationships.

How Do I Show My Customers That I Value Them?

► Keep your promises.

► Treat them with respect.

► Listen to what they actually need, not what you want to sell them.

► Survey your customers to find out how they perceive your company.

Businesses that value the individuals that they work with, in the long run, will likely create a flourishing business that is stronger than the businesses that do not value the people they interact with. Hiring and training new employees is expensive. Vendors who are not treated with respect will increase their prices. The cost to find new customers far outweighs the cost of time to nurture and build long-term relationships with existing customers. The reality? It is just more fun to run a business that respects and values each person.

CHAPTER 8

Operate in Grace

What Does Grace In Business Look Like?

Grace is a word that is seldom used in a business context. Grace engenders the picture of elegance in movement, such as that of a dancer in ballet. Grace is also used in a theological context. Many religions see grace as a divine influence operating in humans to inspire virtuous impulses and impart strength to endure trials. Grace is considered an individual virtue, something that is a desirable trait.

Grace in business means showing this virtue by treating others with respect and dignity. Grace means being encouraging and helpful to your business associates. Grace is a source of positive energy that lifts the spirit of all who it touches. When grace is experienced in a business context, it reflects all that is good about working with people. It means showing civility and etiquette. It takes thoughtfulness and consideration of others. As a core value, operating in grace encapsulates the five core values that have been laid out in previous chapters of this book. Grace is about extraordinary stewardship of authentic relationships developed and operating in integrity, with an attitude of service, placing value on the individual.

> *A company is stronger if bound by love than by fear.*[42]
> —THE LATE HERB KELLEHER, CO-FOUNDER, CEO, AND CHAIRMAN OF SOUTHWEST AIRLINES

A Deeper Dive Into What Grace in Business Looks Like

Grace is best experienced within the context of authentic relationships. When people connect personally in business, there is a better understanding of someone's motivations. Suppose a business associate's decision or behavior rubs you the wrong way. In that case, your reaction to that slight will be dependent on the level and depth of relationship that has been developed. If there is no relationship with your colleague, then the reaction will likely be adverse and self-serving. An authentic relationship will create an environment for listening patiently and allowing for feedback. Genuine relationships allow for grace to be shown with humility by acknowledging our weaknesses and the desire to improve skills. Grace gives one the space to be vulnerable with others, which only deepens trust and relationships. Grace is seen in combining many qualities of how one treats or values others. Grace presents itself by showing respect and treating others with dignity. Grace is encouraging and helping others and creating positive energy with team members. Grace is assisting others to feel good about themselves. We all need grace in our lives at some point.

Operating in grace can be a hard balance to achieve in the business world. Consideration needs to be made between individuals, groups, and the overall financial success of the business. Each of these considerations need to operate with integrity. Businesspeople operate in a highly competitive environment and operating with integrity and grace will take deliberate thoughtfulness and a focus on the core value of grace. When the competition engages in questionable tactics, is grace extended to your employees by not asking them to engage in the same tactics? Do you encourage your employees to stay true to the value of integrity despite what the competition is doing? This would be a picture of extending grace.

Today's fast-paced and high-performance work environments seldom allow for underperformance by individuals. This high pressure can result in employees' hiding mistakes and not taking responsibility for their actions. Creating an environment of grace allows for errors and understands that we all stumble and fall occasionally. Grace seeks to understand why a mistake happened and work on a solution to avoid future mistakes. A safe space is created for the person to admit to mistakes and seek out a solution collaboratively. This deepens relationships and helps build the team spirit to accomplish more together.

Operating in grace means balancing the actions of the individual with the overall good of the team. Extending grace to an individual can turn into enabling that person to the detriment of the team. Tolerating poor behavior in the name of grace is not extending grace to fellow team members. Implementing discipline for actions that are counterproductive to the team goals is operating in grace. Grace is being thoughtful, compassionate, and understanding, but not to try to please people. Taking responsibility for our mistakes while looking for solutions without blaming or shaming is grace in action.

Extending grace to team members should be looked at as strengthening the business. But what about extending grace to vendors, customers, and the general community? The saying "give them an inch and they will take a mile" comes to mind. It can be a hard balance offering grace to business associates and making right business decisions. Perhaps a customer is having a difficult time paying for your product. Do you extend grace or cut them off? A vendor is short on cash and would like you to pay in ten days when your standard credit terms are thirty days. Do you extend grace and pay in the ten days? Are you being taken advantage of, and will this create resentment? There will be times you will have to say "No." There will be times where you say "Yes," and the client does not follow through. In the end, a business owner must proceed with confidence that doing the right thing stems from deeply held core values. When decisions are made that are in violation of one's core values, they seldom turn out for what is best for the company in the long term.

"Treat others as you would like others to treat you" is the principle of grace as articulated in many of the major world religions.

Stories Of Success

"I am closing this business and walking away from the lease. You can deal with it."

I found myself facing large monthly lease payments for a business space that a small sub shop I owned had occupied. I had sold the business a year before to a person who wanted to make the sub shop a lifestyle business. He quit his full-time job and began managing the store immediately. Then the economic recession of 2008 hit. The company started to lose money to the point that it was not sustainable to stay in business.

I was notified by the landlord that the rent had not been paid for several months. I had been forced to keep my name on the lease for the sale of the business to go through and so now the landlord was pursuing me to pay the past due and ongoing rent payments. I immediately went to the store to talk with the owner, and I found that he had closed the doors and walked away without notice. In fact, he had his house on the market and had already moved out of state.

I appealed to the landlord, but I was offered no grace. This store had diligently paid the monthly rent on time for nearly ten years, but this did not sway the landlord to reduce or abate the monthly rent. I paid the past due rent and continued to make the monthly rent payment despite the store being closed.

My options were limited. I began appealing to the landlord to find a new tenant for the spot. His response was to offer it for rent at an increased price, knowing full well that I would be obligated to pay the rent until he found someone willing to pay his price. I then appealed to the listing agent and helped him understand that the rental price was too high to sustain a business and that he would not get his commission if he couldn't find anyone to take over the rent. He dropped the price, and soon a new leaseholder was found. I had to make several concessions to get my name off the lease, but I was eventually free of it.

The next step was to find the business owner that had walked away from the lease and convince him that he owed me the money that I had paid the landlord. His initial response was that he did not think he owed me any money because it was unfair that he had purchased the business just as the recession was beginning. I promptly filed a claim in small claims court to establish the legal precedence that he was responsible for paying me back for the rent payments that I had made on his behalf.

With this ruling in my favor, rather than pursuing the total amount he owed through the legal process, I offered him a deal. I told him that if he chose to ignore my requests to pay back his obligations to me, I would pursue court actions, which would cost him even more money. If he was willing to work with me outside of the court system, he could pay me back over five years with no interest. If he missed any payments, the signed agreement stated I could assess interest from the beginning of the contract until it was completely paid off.

Several people told me that I had been too lenient with this person, and that I should have sued him in court, put a lien on everything he owned, and collected interest and court costs. This was the only way that I could be assured of being paid. I chose to offer grace and dignity to this person instead. He agreed to sign the promissory note and began to make monthly payments. Over the five years, he approached me a couple of times asking to miss a payment because of short-term financial difficulties he was having. Because he always asked for permission, I granted the request. Five years later, the entire amount of $42,000 was paid back, and we each walked away with our integrity knowing we each had done the right thing in the end.

Evidence Of Valuing The Individual

I love the concept of grace in business. It is a wonderful principle. I have worked my whole career with this principle in mind. If I show people they are appreciated, valued, and heard, they inevitably work harder and try their best to live up to expectations. Extending grace gives the gift of dignity. I treat each person as a person and not as an object or asset. Each person I interact with in business, is a person with dreams, feelings, and needs. This is grace in business.

I have found very few examples of grace in business as I researched this topic. Robert Ferguson wrote that he researched all the Fortune 500 companies' value statements, and he did not find a single reference to the value of grace.[43] This is not a surprising revelation. Grace would seem to project weakness and vulnerability. These are not attributes or traits that most businesses would want to be known for. And yet, many of us have likely experienced grace in one form or another over our career. It may not have been acknowledged as such or necessarily endorsed by leadership, but grace still found a way to rise above the quest for profits over people.

There has long been a story circulating inside IBM about Tom Watson, Jr.'s example of extending grace to a company's VP. As the story goes, a VP of IBM was the person overseeing a failed development project that cost IBM $10 million. Tom Watson brought this person into his office to discuss the outcome of the project. The VP, in anticipation of being fired, offered his letter of resignation. But Mr. Watson just shook his head and reportedly said, "Why would I fire you when we just invested $10 million into your education?"

The business world culture is not known for allowing a person to keep their job after making such a costly mistake. Yet, IBM grew to become one of the largest and most successful companies ever by following Mr. Watson's example of using failure as an educational experience rather than a reason to fire someone. This is grace in business.

Mr. Ferguson went on to equate grace to undeserved love. Grace isn't something earned or necessarily deserved, but it is a value that benefits everyone. Imagine for a moment that businesses were known for promoting the value of grace. Grace builds hope in individuals that may feel hopeless working in a harsh dog-eat-dog business environment. Hope brings confidence in how someone approaches their job. Confidence will ignite passion for what a person is doing. Can you imagine how operating in the unconventional practice of extending grace can enhance and accelerate business growth?

In business, as a core value, grace must be modeled by the top leadership in any company to be effective and permeate the organization. Policies and procedures need to be designed to prevent profit from being the only factor in promoting people development. Companies that operate in grace are more values-driven than rules-driven. Rules are important, and people need to know that the company is being fair in how discipline and accountability are implemented. Disagreement among staff will happen, and so dispute resolutions need to be fair within the context of grace.

Operating in grace will be a benefit to an organization. When people feel safe, valued, listened to, and cared for they will bring their best selves forward for the company. Please make no mistake, operating in grace is not a value that naturally plays itself out in business. Leaders of the company will need to model it, invest in it, and commit to it.

APPLICATION

Operating in grace and, dare I say, love in business is not for the faint of heart. The traditional culture of business rarely expresses itself in grace and love. If you are inspired to live out grace and love in the workplace, consider the following actions that demonstrate grace and love in the workplace:

- ▶ Listen to what others are saying.

- ▶ Ask engaging questions.

- ▶ Share information about a project or vision of the company.

- ▶ Be transparent with your team.

- ▶ Reframe challenges as learning opportunities.

- ▶ Support others in their endeavors.

- ▶ Use humor in a positive way.

- ► Be willing to mentor those not as experienced as yourself.

- ► Engage the opinions of others.

- ► Communicate in a clear and caring way.

- ► Take accountability for your actions and decisions.

- ► Invest in people and cheer on people's personal growth.

- ► Celebrate wins together.

Caring for people, acknowledging our weaknesses, treating people with respect and dignity. Is this too much to ask for in business?

CHAPTER 9

Build A Sustainable Business

How do you double your revenue, double your profits, and build a sustainable business? Meet Dan Price, the CEO of Gravity Payments. In 2015, Dan announced that he was raising the minimum wage for everyone working for Gravity to $70,000 per year. He called the move a "moral imperative" to do what he believed was right. It was a move that made headlines around the world. The concept of paying everyone a minimum of $70,000 per year was a controversial idea. Some business owners praised the idea and committed to follow the example in their own business. Other owners were angry that Dan had set the expectation for their own employees that they were underpaid. Some accused Dan of being a socialist, a label that is the antithesis of an entrepreneur in the business world.

Dan's mission is to create a world where values-based companies reshape the economy. He calls on leaders to develop and carry out their own purpose-driven visions by questioning the traditional market-centric business wisdom. Price believes that creating a human focused approach to business, in the long run, will be a much more sustainable model. He has found in his own business, Gravity Payments, that by making this change, a risky prospect, has ultimately helped his company become more resilient and competitive.

Mission critical to building a sustainable business is to build the business based on key values. Identifying and living out these values will drive the vision and culture of the company. Values influence who you work with and how your work is carried out. Great companies are built on great values.

> *It doesn't matter what core values you have. It matters that you have core values, that you preserve them over time, that you are passionately committed to them, and that you align your behaviors and your organizational practices and structures and strategies with those core values.*[44]

> —Jim Collins

The Noble CFO has six core values that drive who a CFO Business Partner works with, how that work is accomplished, and why the Partners do the work they do. When a business associate refers a prospective client to the firm, the first response is to ask for an introduction to meet the business owner. The interview is not to sell the services of CFO Business Partner, but to determine if there is a values alignment. The scope of work is identified based on the prospect's need, not a predetermined template.

The six core values of *The Noble CFO* have guided CFO Business Partner for the past eight years. The business has expanded every year, primarily by adding new clients in addition to maintaining existing clients. New clients come exclusively through referrals from existing clients and long-term business associates. The foundation of the business is the values that are lived out. The outcome of basing the company on these values is to continue to serve existing clients and develop new clients from business associates who see CFO Business Partner as a trusted partner.

Successful Executive Turned Entrepreneur

Doug was a successful marketing executive for several high-tech firms in the Seattle area. He had helped the business owners launch and grow their organizations into successful fixtures in the business community. Like many employees, Doug saw that most of his work's financial fruit was bestowed upon the business owners. He was pleased that his diligent work produced financial success for the owners and that he was rewarded financially. However, this experience motivated him to consider launching his own business. He knew how to market and grow a business, had a passion for sports, and was looking for a way to combine the two into a successful enterprise.

The opportunity to purchase the rights to market the iconic Electric Football game became available, and Doug, with the investor's backing, purchased the business. Tudor Games, as the company was called, accelerated in growth, demanding a higher level of inventory. Doug went to the bank to inquire about getting a loan to fund inventory and provide operating funds. It was clear from the questions that the bank asked that the company needed someone to provide a higher level of accounting and finance expertise than what Doug himself could provide.

Doug began to ask business associates for recommendations on what was the best way to address this deficit. He knew the business could not afford the cost of a full-time accountant or CFO, but that was the level of expertise he needed. Michelle, the banker he had worked with to obtain the loan, recommended hiring a contracted CFO on a part-time basis to provide the support he needed. Michelle, per bank policy, gave Doug three different names to consider for the role. Doug interviewed each person to let them know he was interested in hiring a part-time CFO and that they were one of three that were under consideration.

CFO Business Partner was one of the three CFOs who was being considered for the position. I put together a proposal that clearly stated my experience and the type of deliverables that Doug could expect. I knew that this was not going to be the differentiator in Doug's decision. Michelle would not have made the three recommendations unless she knew that all three were qualified for the position.

Doug and I met for coffee to discuss my proposal. My attention was on connecting with Doug on a personal level. I provided some history on who I was and what my experiences were. I emphasized the values that I believed in and how these values were reflected in my life and work history. Doug and I both felt that there was an alignment of values after our meeting. A day later, Doug called me and told me I had the job.

The journey with Doug and Tudor Games has had its ups and downs. Projecting inventory purchases in the summer, based on anticipated sales for Christmas, is not easy. Purchasing too much inventory caused cash shortages in the spring and summer when sales dropped off. Purchasing too little inventory would result in running out of product, with no way to fulfill backorders on a timely basis.

There have been times where Doug just needed to have someone to talk with and express his doubts and concerns. I was always there to listen and offer encouragement. Our common values are what has held the relationship together for this many years. Without that alignment, we both might have given up on Tudor Games.

Today, Tudor Games continues to grow and is now looking to expand its product line through a new partner. Doug trusts that I have his best interests in mind as we consider this new partnership and the best way to market new products because of our authentic relationship. I have earned the trust because I have always operated in integrity and pursued extraordinary stewardship over the business. We have both made mistakes over the years, but we both operate in grace, learn from our mistakes, and genuinely desire to serve each other's interests. The words of Jim Collins (*Good to Great*, 2001) are worth repeating: "It doesn't matter what core values you have. It matters that you have core values, that you preserve them over time, that you are passionately committed to them, and that you align your behaviors and your organizational practices and structures and strategies with those core values."

Formal business education and practice focus on bringing the maximum return on shareholders and business owners' investment. The myth is that profit is the ultimate purpose of owning a business. Profit or loss are simply outcomes of operating a business. History has shown us many examples of companies that operated solely to maximize profits and got caught up in scandals and compromising business decisions. Standard Oil, TWA, Enron, Lincoln Savings and Loan, E.F. Hutton, Arthur Andersen, WorldCom, Tyco International, Bear Stearns, Lehman Brothers—you get the picture. The list of CFOs who have gone to jail because they either had no values or compromised their values to meet the demand of increasing profits is long as well. Most of the companies listed above had their finance chiefs go to jail. Profit should never trump values in the business world.

Unfortunately, the companies that spectacularly fail because of corruption and a sole focus on profits make the headlines. What about business success stories? These stories may be harder to find, but they are out there. In his books *Good To Great* and *Built to Last* (New York: Harper Business, 1994), Jim Collins describes several businesses that operated on a values-based premise. Costco has been a phenomenal success as well. They are profitable, their employees are loyal, and their customers love them. Costco had four values, which they called a code of ethics: 1) Obey the Law 2) Take care of our members 3) Take care of our employees 4) Respect our vendors.[45] These values set the foundation for a successful, well-loved business. Jim Sinegal, the founder of Costco, said, "Culture isn't the most important thing; it's the only thing." Zappos is another wildly successful company that built its success on ten core values. The values are personal, meaningful, and unique to that business. The values tell you what this business stands for. Gravity Payments, as noted earlier in this chapter, had core values that reflected service and value of the individual. Dan Price valued his employees and believed that every employee should be making a livable wage. He has doubled his revenue and profit.

The evidence is clear for these companies that having core values as the foundation of the business drives them to success. A clearly written and communicated set of core values enables employees to make decisions that benefit the company with onerous oversight. These values need to be lived out in the company culture throughout the organization. If the leaders do not follow the values, the rest of the employees will not follow the values, and the customers will sense the dissonance between words and actions. Today's entrepreneurs are changing the business world. Innovation and solutions built on values are the future of business. Companies that stand on values today will be the business leaders of tomorrow.

Entrepreneurs and business owners want to build a sustainable business. I am convinced that the critical piece of building a long-term sustainable business is to lay a foundation of core values from which to operate. Here are some simple points to consider in effort to accomplish this objective:

1. Identify your core values. This would appear to be an obvious suggestion, but many people have not gone through the exercise of understanding and writing down what is most important to them. Take time to consider how you have responded to people and actions in the past. What has caused you to say that this is what I believe in, or this is an area that I simply will not tolerate in my life? Write out your thoughts and begin to hone them into several essential values in your life.

2. Define your values. When you say integrity is a core value, what does that mean for you? Provide some narrative around the definition of a particular core value. Words have different meanings to different people depending on their context.

3. Write out examples of how your core value is lived out in your life. It will be easier for others to

understand what your core value means to you when you are able to show examples of living that value.

4. Align yourself with other individuals that reflect your values. There is strength in partnerships and collaboration. Finding the people you align with will make your journey to follow your values that much easier.

5. Communicate your values with clarity. Once you have decided on what values are important to you, take the opportunity to share these values with others. The more people understand who you are and what you stand for, the more likely they are to support you and do business with you.

6. Attract others to your core values. When you are prospecting for new clients, or networking with business associates, wear your values on your sleeve. Do not let the opportunity pass without sharing your values in some way.

7. Open up yourself to be accountable. The more you share and live your values, the more people will expect to see these values lived out in your life. Being consistent in living out your values will reinforce the importance of them.

CHAPTER 10

Into the Future

Imagine a world where nearly 50 percent of U.S. workers participate in the gig economy doing freelance, contract, temporary, or independent contractor work. Now further imagine that the majority of business owners in this world are committed to building values-driven organizations. This is the future of global and local business.

The story of the U.S. worker over the past decade has been one of change and adjustments. Coming out of the Great Recession we have seen technological and societal shifts in how business is conducted and how employees engage with their employer. The Pew Research Center Study has noted several changes having an impact on today's worker.[46] The trend of an aging population carries over to the workforce where Americans over fifty-five years of age make up a fifth of the total labor force. These workers are also staying in the workforce longer, which creates less advancement opportunities for mid-career people.

The study also found that the time an unemployed person remains out of work has gotten longer. This trend has accelerated with the pandemic of 2020 and 2021. The jobs that are available in the U.S. economy have continued to shift to jobs that are classified as service oriented. The higher-paying manufacturing jobs are disappearing as automation reduces the need for workers and manufacturing is outsourced to other parts of the world.

The U.S. worker is resilient and so this is not the end of the story. The trend towards service jobs is creating new opportunities. Workers are realizing that there is no such thing as job security, and they have been honing their skills and learning new skills. Many of these skills include consulting and contract work in industries employees are familiar with. The risk of being downsized or laid off is being mitigated with the focus on the gig economy.

The newfound independence that comes with working in the gig economy as a consultant or contract worker opens the opportunity to find values-based companies to partner with. With more people insisting on only partnering or working for companies that align with their own values, businesses are coming to the realization that to fill needed roles they must adjust to this new economy as well. This is all good news for the worker who is willing to look to the future and take advantage of the shift from hiring long-term W-2 employees to outsourcing support and service roles to successful consultants and contract workers.

Adapting to the new reality of the gig economy is not for the faint-hearted. If you have been working as a W-2 employee for any number of years, you likely have become dependent on the "safety" of full-time employment. There are paid vacations and holidays as benefits. The cost of health care insurance coverage has become increasingly expensive and knowing you participate in a company-sponsored plan provides some comfort that a major illness will not bankrupt you. You have an office and company-owned office equipment. Technology issues are covered by an in-house expert or at least the outsourced IT person is paid for by the company. Walking away from these comforts and benefits is not easy. I have friends who continue to work for companies that they hate but are not able to convince themselves to leave for something that may or may not be better. All of that is true and you might ask yourself, "Can I just last another ten or fifteen years until retirement as a W-2 employee?" I do not know the answer to that question. I do know that the gig economy has become a mainstay of the U.S. economy. The freelance economy is growing much faster than the traditional workforce. Companies are looking at ways to reduce their employee counts by eliminating support roles that are not directly related to the product or service that they sell. W-2 employment is no longer a guaranteed path to a comfortable retirement.

Today is the day to begin planning for the new economy. Evaluate your work experience from the perspective of how you have been able to add value to a company. What expertise have you developed? How can you leverage that expertise in a way that prepares you to enter the gig economy? Who is in your network of business associates? What advice and help are they able to provide as you consider a consulting career? Are your finances in a place that will allow you to jump full-time into a freelance position? Or do you need to make a slower transition to build up a side income in advance of going full-time? Do you have the support of your family and significant other? These are the practical considerations in contemplating entering the gig economy.

I believe that as important as the practical considerations listed above are, it is equally important to understand your personal values. When you face difficult decisions, what are the values that keep you grounded to be able to make choices that you will not regret? What values drive you to continue moving forward when times are tough? How do your values align with the prospective clients you are talking with? If your client has values that run counter to your personal values, you will stay in a state of tension and unease. You will not enjoy your work and you will likely add less value to the business than what is expected.

CFO Business Partner has established six values that are non-negotiable in how a noble CFO operates in the business world. These values are not intended to be all-inclusive for every person in every situation. They are also not intended to communicate that everyone should have the same set of values, or that they are the best values for a business to follow. These values are what make CFO Business Partner unique. When a client engages with CFO Business Partner, they can expect to see these values lived out in the work that is done and the relationships that develop.

Developing authentic relationships has multiple benefits for your business and the rest of your life. Business leaders realize that authentic relationships are a vital element in building trust with employees and customers. Trust and connection are outcomes of vulnerability in relationships. Investing in relationships is time well spent. Developing authentic relationships is a long-term strategy. When a connection is formed and matured with the right people, the return on that investment will far exceed the value focusing on one-time transactions. Long-term relationships are nurtured over the years. The financial benefit comes from providing a service or product that is truly needed and desired by your customer and not based on a perceived need.

Developing relationships might not always show up in the form of money but could lead to your personal growth or opportunities outside of the business. Investing in authentic relationships with your time, resources, connections, and expertise will lead to a richer and more rewarding life and business.

Integrity is the most valuable and respected quality of leadership. Integrity is the quality of being honest and having strong moral principles. There are many stories in society and businesses of people who struggle with making an ethical decision when faced with intense pressure to act in a way that is unethical. Internalizing an established code of ethics and then being honest in living out that code is how integrity is maintained.

Integrity is a state of mind and is not situational. If you compromise your integrity in small situations with little consequence, it becomes easy to compromise on larger cases. Leaders with integrity always err on the side of fairness, especially when other people are being unfair. The internalization of integrity allows you to be fair when other people are mistreating you.

Integrity in business is an essential ingredient for sustainable, long-term business growth, and success. It can be hard to define and difficult to measure, but you know it when you see it, and it is clear when it is not there. Always keep your word and operate with the best interest of others in mind.

Stewardship is about service to something greater. Stewardship asks us to be deeply accountable for our organizations' outcomes without trying to control others or trying to take care of them. It requires a redistribution of power by giving away power to those who may have the least "important" position in a company to make decisions.

Service over self-interest runs entirely counter to the way most business leaders have been trained and yet this is a vital part of creating an environment of extraordinary business stewardship. Trusting and believing that every person is created to make decisions and will, if given the opportunity, make decisions that benefit the community or organization over self, lays the foundation for a transformational stewardship environment.

Long-term sustainability of a business depends on the proper balance of stewarding profits, people, and the community. There is power in unity and the collective efforts of business and community. So much more can be accomplished in the community when stewardship of place focuses on the business community. Supporting the civic, education, nonprofit, and faith sectors of the community is also good for business.

Pursuing an attitude of service runs counter to what most management and leadership books have taught in the past. The servant-leader is the person who has a natural desire to put others' interests before their own. They are driven by the desire to see others grow and develop as people and workers to their greatest potential. They are willing to put aside their own goals to help others accomplish their purposes. They live a life of integrity where they say what they do, and do what they say, both at work and at home.

Pursuing an attitude of service is a characteristic of some highly successful companies. They have a people-focused culture that ensures meaningful stability during times of rapid change. Many business thinkers and writers recognize the value of servant-leadership. The attitude is increasingly relevant to the challenges in today's business.

The fundamental importance of democracy is that each individual matters. No matter what walk of life a person comes from, each opinion and voice is unique. A business should treat every individual it interacts with, in a way that values their dignity and worth. When a company values the individual employee the criteria for organizational performance and success is not measured primarily in financial terms, but rather that the workplace is filled with joy for the ordinary worker and is measured by the worker's quality of life. Engaged and happy employees will be more productive and add to a company's bottom line.

Grace is considered an individual virtue, something that is a desirable trait. Grace in business means showing this virtue by treating others with respect and dignity. Grace is best experienced within the context of authentic relationships. Genuine relationships allow for grace to be shown with humility by acknowledging our weaknesses and the desire to improve skills. Grace gives one the space to be vulnerable with others, which only deepens trust and relationships.

Grace would seem to project weakness and vulnerability. These are not attributes or traits that most businesses would want to be known for. And yet many of us have likely experienced grace in one form or another over our career. It may not have been acknowledged as such or necessarily endorsed by leadership, but grace still found a way to rise above the quest for profits over people. Operating in grace is not a value that naturally plays itself out in business, yet it will be a benefit to any organization.

The world is rapidly changing all around us. Looking back a mere thirty years, we see the fall of the Berlin Wall which was the end of the Cold War. This was the start of the globalization of business. The internet and the advance of technology has exponentially changed the business environment and how business is conducted. The Great Recession, social unrest, and the COVID-19 pandemic have had a profound impact on highlighting the widening wealth gap. What does this mean for the future of business? How can we prepare for the inevitable changes that are ahead of us?

I see two trends that are affecting business in a way that makes engaging in a consulting business a smart move. The first trend is the growth of the gig economy. There have been many studies and surveys that look at the statistics and facts[47] on this growing trend. The future of business is moving in this direction and like most things in life, the sooner one takes advantage of a growing trend the better positioned you will be.

The second trend is the widening gap between the rich and the poor and the resulting business trend of creating values-driven company cultures. This may not seem an obvious reason to move towards establishing a consulting business, but there will be a social revolution at some level as a result of this widening gap. Companies that establish and live out the values that are people and community friendly are going to be the businesses that will flourish in this environment. As a consultant, operating with these values, your impact will be multiplied.

This is an exciting time to take control of your time, income, and business environment. The opportunity is now. Take the risk and join me in becoming a Noble CFO.

About The Author

A rt Zylstra, MBA, DTL is a seasoned and highly respected CFO. He is the founder of CFO Business Partner, a company that works with owners of for-profit and non-profit organizations to help them flourish and grow. With his M.B.A. in Organizational Leadership and his Doctorate in Transformational Leadership, Art is well-equipped to collaborate with key members of an executive team and develop and implement key strategies across the organization.

Art is highly motivated by mission and operates with integrity, confidence, professionalism, and resourcefulness. The passion that fuels Art is the understanding that when privately held businesses steward their profits, people, partners. and places in extraordinary ways, the businesses and the community flourish.

It is Art's mission in life to help as many businesses as possible to grow and thrive in a way that helps the community flourish. Art coaches other CFOs under the brand of CFO Business Partner to extend this influence throughout the country.

Art was raised on a dairy farm in Western Washington and developed a strong work ethic that has influenced his career and volunteer work. Art has served on a variety of boards over the years and currently serves on two boards in his hometown, one as Treasurer and one as President.

Art loves to travel and spend time with his wife, three children, and six grandchildren. His travels have brought him to five different continents on multiple occasions.

To work with Art directly as your CFO, or to become a CFO under the CFO Business Partner brand, please email the author at ArtZ@CFOBusinessPartner.com For those interested in having Art speak to your company, organization or podcast please, email Art at Art@TheNobleCFO.com.

ENDNOTES

1. Steve Jobs, "'You've got to find what you love,' Jobs says", *News. stanford.edu*, June 14, 2005, Accessed March 13, 2021, https://news.stanford.edu/2005/06/14/jobs-061505/.

2. "The Characteristics of Those in the Gig Economy", *Gov.uk*, February 7, 2018, Accessed March 24, 2021, https://assets. publishing.service.gov.uk/government/uploads/system/uploads/ attachment_data/file/687553/The_characteristics_of_those_in_ the_gig_economy.pdf.

3. Eden McCallum, "Independent Consulting: A Good Gig in a Changing World", *Edenmccallum.com*, October 2018, Accessed February 14, 2021, https://edenmccallum.com/wp-content/ uploads/securepdfs/2019/05/survey-report.pdf.

4. William Miller, "Death of a Genius: His Fourth Dimension, Time", *Life,* May 2, 1955, 62-64.

5. Leanne Jacobs, *Goodreads.com*, Accessed February 3, 2021 https://www.goodreads.com/quotes/9646969-if-an-opportunity-is-not-aligned-with-that-matters-most.

6. Charles H. Green and David H. Maister, *The Trusted Advisor*, (New York, NY: Touchstone, 2001).

7. Alice Schroeder, *The Snowball: Warren Buffett and the Business of Life*, (New York: Bantam Books, 2008)

8. Jim Collins, *Good to Great: Why Some Companies Make It and Others Don't,* (New York, NY: HarperCollins, 2001).

9. Journal of Neuroscience, "Amygdala Responsivity to High-Level Social Information from Unseen Faces", *Jneurosci.org*. August 6, 2014, Accessed January 5, 2021, https://www.jneurosci.org/ content/34/32/10573.

10. Olivier Serrat, "Understanding and Developing Emotional Intelligence," Springer Link, May 23, 2017, https://link.springer.com/chapter/10.1007/978-981-10-0983-9_37#Fn3_source.

11. Brene Brown, "The Power of Vulnerability", Filmed June 2010 in Houston, TX, TED Video, 20:03, https://www.ted.com/talks/brene_brown_the_power_of_vulnerability.

12. Bradley J. Sugars, *Instant Sales*, (New York: McGraw-Hill Educational, 2006).

13. Forbes Insights, "The Case for Face-to-Face Meetings," *Forbes,* 2009, Accessed December 15, 2020, https://images.forbes.com/forbesinsights/StudyPDFs/Business_Meetings_FaceToFace.pdf.

14. Nuria K. Mackes, Dennis Golma, Owen G. O'Daly, Sagar Sarkar, Edmund J.S .Sonuga-Barke, Graeme Fairchild, Mitul A. Mehtab, "Tracking Emotions in the Brain—Revisiting the Empathic Accuracy Task", *NeuroImage*, Volume 178, September 2018, 677-686, Accessed March 21, 2021, https://www.ncbi.nlm.nih.gov/pmc/articles/PMC6057276/.

15. Barbara L. Fredrickson *Love 2.0: How Our Supreme Emotion Affects Everything We Feel, Think, Do, and Become*, (New York, NY: Plume, 2014).

16. *Oxford Learners Dictionary*, "integrity (*n.*)," accessed April 6, 2019. https://www.oxfordlearnersdictionaries.com/definition/english/integrity?q=integrity

17. Brian Tracy, "Critical Success Factor: Developing A Moral Character To Achieve Greatness," *Briantracy.com* (blog), Accessed March 29, 2021, https://www.briantracy.com/blog/personal-success/success-factor-moral-character-a-good-person/.

18. Warren Buffett said after Solomon Brothers scandal in 1991.

19. Brian Tracy, "The Importance of Honesty and Integrity in Business," *Briantracy.com*, https://www.briantracy.com/blog/leadership-success/importance-of-honesty-integrity-in-business.

20. Fredrickson, *Love 2.0.*

21. Alec Mackenzie, *The Time Trap: The Classic Book on Time Management*, (New York: Amacon, 1990).

22. Stephen R. Covey, *Principle-Centered Leadership*, (New York: Rosetta Books, 2009).

23. Peter Block, *Stewardship: Choosing Service Over Self-Interest*, (Oakland, CA: Berrett-Koehler Publishers, 2013), 6.

24. Block, *Stewardship*, 7.

25. Christopher Ingraham, "The richest 1 percent now owns more of the country's wealth than at any time in the past 50 years," *Washington Post*, December 6, 2017, Accessed December 20, 2020, https://www.washingtonpost.com/news/wonk/wp/2017/12/06/the-richest-1-percent-now-owns-more-of-the-countrys-wealth-than-at-any-time-in-the-past-50-years/.

26. Christopher Ingraham, "Nation's top 1 percent now have greater wealth than the bottom 90 percent," *Seattle Times*, December 8, 2017, https://www.seattletimes.com/business/economy/nations-top-1-percent-now-have-greater-wealth-than-the-bottom-90-percent/.

27. Ingraham, Nation's top 1 percent.

28. Josh Spiro, "Are Your Employees Scared to Take Vacation?" *Inc.com*, January 8, 2010, https://www.inc.com/news/articles/2010/01/vacation-policy.html

29. Robert K. Greenleaf, Hamilton Beazley, Julie Beggs, and Larry C. Spears. *The Servant-Leader Within: A Transformative Path* (New York: Paulist Press, 2003), 16.

30. James W. Sipe, and Don M. Frick, *Seven Pillars of Servant Leadership: Practicing the Wisdom of Leading by Serving*, (New York, NY: Paulist Press, 2009), 4.

31. Andy Stanley, *Visioneering: Your Guide for Discovering and Maintaining Personal Vision*, (Sisters, OR: Multnomah Publishers, 2016), 9-12.

32. Kenneth H. Blanchard, and Phil Hodges. *The Servant Leader: Transforming Your Heart, Head, Hands, and Habits.* (Nashville, TN: J. Countryman, 2003), 68.

33. Tom Peters, "Organizations Exist to Serve: Why Else Get Out of Bed in the Morning?", *Tompeters.com*, May 29, 2014, https://tompeters.com/wpcontent/uploads/2014/02/Exist_to_serve_052914.pdf.

34. Simon Sinek, *Leaders Eat Last; Why Some Teams Pull Together, and Some Don't,* (London: Portfolio Publishers, 2014).

35. "7 Servant Leadership Examples in Business (Some May Surprise You!)," *SkillPacks.com*, December 29, 2020, https://www.skillpacks.com/servant-leadership-examples-in-business/.

36. Peter Ferdinand Drucker, *"Classic Drucker: Essential Wisdom of Peter Drucker from the Pages of Harvard Business Review"* (Boston: Harvard Business Press, 2006), 59.

37. Robert Greenleaf, "What is Servant-Leadership?" *Greenleaf.com*, 2017, https://www.greenleaf.org/what-is-servant-leadership/.

38. "State of the Global Workplace," Annual Report, New York, NY: Gallup Press, 2017.

39. Josh Spiro, "Are Your Employees Scared to Take Vacation?", *Inc.com*, January 8, 2010, https://www.inc.com/news/articles/2010/01/vacation-policy.html.

40. "The Vendor Client Relationship." *Changefactory.com*, Accessed February 19, 2021, https://www.changefactory.com.au/our-thinking/articles/the-vendor-client-relationship-educate-each-other-and-benefit/.

41. Renate Cunneen, "The Biggest Mistake Clients Make When Dealing with Outsourced Vendors." *The Huffington Post*", *TheHuffingtonPost.com*, December 7, 2017. https://www.huffpost.com/entry/the-biggest-mistake-clien_b_9817852.

42. Herb Kelleher Quotes. *BrainyQuote.com*, Brainy Media Inc, 2021. https://www.brainyquote.com/quotes/herb_kelleher_307784, Accessed March 21, 2021.

43. "The Secret Power Of Grace." *Fergusonvalues.com*, Accessed February 19, 2021. https://www.fergusonvalues.com/2015/12/the-secret-power-of-grace/.

44. Jim Collins, "It Really Matters That You Have Core Values. It Really Doesn't Matter What They Are!" *Jimcollins.com*, 2017, Accessed February 14, 2021, https://www.jimcollins.com/media_topics/ItReallyMatters.html.

45. "What is Costco's Mission Statement and Code of Ethics?" *Costco.com*, Accessed March 21, 2021, https://customerservice.costco.com/app/answers/detail/a_id/829/~/what-is-costcos-mission-statement-and-code-of-ethics%3F.

46. Drew DeSilver, "5 Ways the U.S. Workforce has Changed, a Decade Since the Great Recession Began 2017," *Pewresearch.org*, November 30, 2017, Accessed December 20, 2020, https://www.pewresearch.org/fact-tank/2017/11/30/5-ways-the-u-s-workforce-has-changed-a-decade-since-the-great-recession-began/.

47. I. Mitic, "24+ Crucial Gig Economy Statistics and Facts," *Fortunly.com*, February 12, 2021, https://fortunly.com/statistics/gig-economy-statistics and I. Mitic "Gig Economy Statistics: The New Normal in the Workplace." *Fortunly.com*, February 12, 2021, https://fortunly.com/statistics/gig-economy-statistics.

BIBLIOGRAPHY

Blanchard, Kenneth H. and Phil Hodges. *The Servant Leader: Transforming Your Heart, Head, Hands, and Habits.* Nashville, TN: J. Countryman, 2003.

Block, Peter, *Stewardship: Choosing Service Over Self-Interest*, Oakland, CA: Berrett-Koehler Publishers, 2013.

Brown, Brene. *The Power of Vulnerability.* Filmed June 2010 in Houston, TX. TED Video. 20:03. https://www.ted.com/talks/brene_brown_the_power_of_vulnerability.

"The Characteristics of Those in the Gig Economy." *Gov.uk.* February 7, 2018. Accessed March 24, 2021. https://assets.publishing.service.gov.uk/government/uploads/system/uploads/attachment_data/file/687553/The_characteristics_of_those_in_the_gig_economy.pdf.

Collins, Jim. *Good To Great: Why Some Companies Make It and Others Do Not.* New York, NY: HarperCollins, 2001.

Collins, Jim. *It Really Matters That You Have Core Values. It Really Doesn't Matter What They Are! Jimcollins.com* (audio). 03.22. Accessed March 21, 2021. https://www.jimcollins.com/media_topics/ItReallyMatters.html.

Costco. "What is Costco's Mission Statement and Code of Ethics?" Costco.com. Accessed March 21, 2021. https://customerservice.costco.com/app/answers/detail/a_id/829/~/what-is-costcos-mission-statement-and-code-of-ethics%3F.

Covey, Steven R. *Principle-Centered Leadership.* New York, NY: Summit Books, 1990.

Department for Business, Energy & Industrial Strategy. "The Characteristics of Those in the Gig Economy." Gov.uk. February 7, 2018. https://assets.publishing.service.gov.uk/government/uploads/

system/uploads/attachment_data/file/687553/The_characteristics_of_those_in_the_gig_economy.pdf

Desilver, Drew. "5 Ways the U.S. Workforce has Changed, a Decade Since the Great Recession Began 2017." *Pewresearch.org.* November 30, 2017. Accessed December 20, 2020. https://www.pewresearch.org/fact-tank/2017/11/30/5-ways-the-u-s-workforce-has-changed-a-decade-since-the-great-recession-began/.

Drucker, Peter Ferdinand. *"Classic Drucker: Essential Wisdom of Peter Drucker from the Pages of Harvard Business Review."* Boston: Harvard Business Press, 2006.

Forbes Insights. "Business Meetings: The Case for Face-to-Face." *Forbes.com.* 2019. Accessed December 15, 2021. https://images.forbes.com/forbesinsights/StudyPDFs/Business_Meetings_FaceToFace.pdf.

Fredrickson, Dr. Barbara. *Love 2.0: How Our Supreme Emotion Affects Everything We Feel, Think, Do, and Become.* New York, NY: Plume, 2014.

Green, Charles H. and David H. Maister *The Trusted Advisor.* New York, NY: Touchstone, 2017.

Greenleaf, Robert, Hamilton Beazley, Julie Beggs, and Larry C. Spears. *The Servant-Leader Within: A Transformative Path.* New York, NY: Paulist Press, 2003.

Greenleaf, Robert. "What is Servant Leadership?" *Greenleaf.org.* 2017. Accessed January 14, 2021. https://www.greenleaf.org/what-is-servant-leadership/.

Ingraham, Christopher. "Nation's top 1 percent now have greater wealth than the bottom 90 percent." *Seattle Times.* December 8, 2017. https://www.seattletimes.com/business/economy/nations-top-1-percent-now-have-greater-wealth-than-the-bottom-90-percent/.

Ingraham, Christopher. "The richest 1 percent now owns more of the country's wealth than at any time in the past 50 years." *Washington Post*, December 6, 2017. https://www.washingtonpost.com/news/

wonk/wp/2017/12/06/the-richest-1-percent-now-owns-more-of-the-countrys-wealth-than-at-any-time-in-the-past-50-years/.

Jacobs, Leanne. Popular Quotes. *Goodreads.com*. Accessed March 21, 2021. https://www.goodreads.com/quotes/9646969-if-an-opportunity-is-not-aligned-with-that-matters-most.

Journal of Neuroscience. "Amygdala Responsivity to High-Level Social Information from Unseen Faces." *Jneurosci.org*. August 6, 2014. https://www.jneurosci.org/content/34/32/10573.

Jobs, Steve. *'You've got to find what you love,' Jobs says." Stanford.edu*. June 14, 2005 Accessed March 13, 2021. https://news.stanford.edu/2005/06/14/jobs-061505/.

Kelleher, Herb. Quotes. *Brainyquote.com*. Brainy Media Inc, 2021. Accessed March 21, 2021. https://www.brainyquote.com/quotes/herb_kelleher_307784.

McCallum, Eden. "Independent Consulting: A Good Gig in a Changing World." *Edenmccallum.com*. October 2018. https://edenmccallum.com/wp-content/uploads/securepdfs/2019/05/survey-report.pdf.

Mackenzie, Alec. *The Time Trap: The Classic Book on Time Management*. New York, NY: Amacon,1990.

Miller, William. "Death of a Genius: His Fourth Dimension, Time." *Life*. May 2, 1955.

Mitic, I. "24+ Crucial Gig Economy Statistics and Facts," *Fortunly.com*. February 12, 2021. https://fortunly.com/statistics/gig-economy-statistics.

Mitic, I. "Gig Economy Statitics: The New Normal in the Workplace." *Fortunly.com*. February 12, 2021. Accessed March 1, 2021. https://fortunly.com/statistics/gig-economy-statistics.

Peters, Tom. "Organizations Exist to Serve: Why Else Get Out of Bed in the Morning?" *Tompeters.com*. May 29, 2014. Accessed January 2, 2021 https://tompeters.com/wpcontent/uploads/2014/02/Exist_to_serve_052914.pdf.

Schroeder, Alice. *The Snowball: Warren Buffett and the Business of Life.* New York, NY: Bantam Books, 2008.

"The Secret Power Of Grace." *Fergusonvalues.com*, Accessed February 19, 2021. https://www.fergusonvalues.com/2015/12/the-secret-power-of-grace/.

Serrat, Olivier. "Understanding and Developing Emotional Intelligence." *Springer Link.* May 23, 2017. https://link.springer.com/chapter/10.1007/978-981-10-0983-9_37#Fn3_source.

"7 Servant Leadership Examples in Business (Some May Surprise You!)." *Skillpacks.com.* December 29, 2020. https://www.skillpacks.com/servant-leadership-examples-in-business/.

Sipe, James W. and Don M. Frick. *Seven Pillars of Servant Leadership: Practicing the Wisdom of Leading by Serving.* New York, NY: Paulist Press, 2009.

Spiro, Josh. "Are Your Employees Scared to Take Vacation?", *Inc.com.* January 8, 2010. https://www.inc.com/news/articles/2010/01/vacation-policy.html.

Stanley, Andy. *Visioneering: Your Guide for Discovering and Maintaining Personal Vision.* Sisters, OR: Multnomah Publishers, 2016.

"State of the Global Workplace" Annual Report. New York, NY: Gallup Press, 2017.

Sugars, Bradley J. *Instant Sales.* New York, NY: McGraw-Hill Educational, 2006.

"Tracking Emotions in the Brain—Revisiting the Empathic Accuracy Task." *National Institute of Health.* September 2018. https://www.ncbi.nlm.nih.gov/pmc/articles/PMC6057276/.

Tracy, Brian. "Critical Success Factor: Developing A Moral Character To Achieve Greatness," *Personal Success* (blog). Accessed March 29, 2021. https://www.briantracy.com/blog/personal-success/success-factor-moral-character-a-good-person/.

Tracy, Brian. "The Importance of Honesty and Integrity in Business." *Leadership Success* (blog). Accessed January 2021. https://www. briantracy.com/blog/leadership-success/importance-of-honesty-integrity-in-business/.

"The Vendor Client Relationship." *Changefactory.com.* Accessed February 19, 2021. https://www.changefactory.com.au/our-thinking/ articles/the-vendor-client-relationship-educate-each-other-and-benefit/.